UBUNTU

LEARN THE VARIOUS ASPECTS OF THE UBUNTU OPERATING SYSTEM AND THE BASICS OF UBUNTU DESKTOPS AND SEVER EDITION

DENNIS HUTTEN

i

UBUNTU TUTORIAL

This tutorial looks at the various aspects of the Ubuntu Operating system. It discusses various features, flavors, and working of the Ubuntu desktop edition. A comparison is made against software which we would normally find on a Windows operating system. There are chapters that focus on the server version of Ubuntu. This tutorial also includes separate chapters for those who are interested in understanding the virtual machines and cloud aspects of Ubuntu.

AUDIENCE

Ubuntu Linux has been around for quite some time in the industry. This tutorial will be beneficial for those who want to learn some basic concepts of the Ubuntu desktop and server edition.

PREREQUISITES

You should be familiar with a basic operating system such as Windows and the various programs that are already available on the Windows operating system.

TABLE OF CONTENTS

Ubuntu - Overview

Ubuntu is a Linux-based operating system. It is designed for computers, smartphones, and network servers. The system is developed by a UK based company called Canonical Ltd. All the principles used to develop the Ubuntu software are based on the principles of Open Source software development.

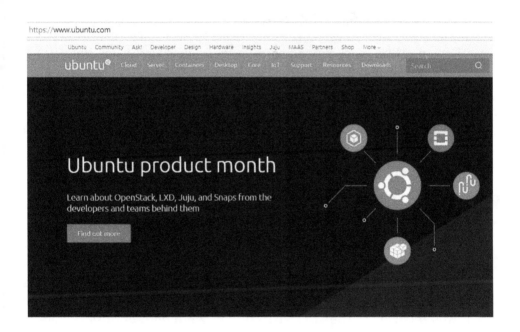

FEATURES OF UBUNTU

Following are some of the significant features of Ubuntu −

- The desktop version of Ubuntu supports all the normal software on Windows such as Firefox, Chrome, VLC, etc.
- It supports the office suite called LibreOffice.
- Ubuntu has an in-built email software called Thunderbird, which gives the user access to email such as Exchange, Gmail, Hotmail, etc.
- There are a host of free applications for users to view and edit photos.
- There are also applications to manage videos and it also allows the users to share videos.
- It is easy to find content on Ubuntu with the smart searching facility.
- The best feature is, it is a free operating system and is backed by a huge open source community.

RELEASE CYCLE OF UBUNTU

Every year there are 2 releases of Ubuntu, one in April and one in October, from Canonical. The version number normally denotes the year in which the software was released. For example, version 14.04 specifies that it was released in the year 2014 and in the month of April. Similarly, the version 16.04 specifies that it was released in the year 2016 and in the month of April. The April build every year is the more stable build, while the October build does a lot of experimentation on new features.

The official site for Ubuntu is https://www.ubuntu.com/

The site has all information and documentation about the Ubuntu Software. It also has the download links for both the server and desktop versions of Ubuntu.

Ubuntu - Flavors

Ubuntu comes in a variety of flavors. In this chapter, we will discuss briefly about some of the popular flavors of Ubuntu.

Ubuntu Desktop

This is the operating system which can be used by regular users. This comes pre-built with software that help the users perform usual basic activities. Operations such as browsing, email and multimedia are also available in this edition. The latest version as of September 2016 is 16.04.01.

Ubuntu Server

The server version is used for hosting applications such as web servers and databases. Each server version is supported by Ubuntu for 5 years. These operating systems have support for cloud platforms such as AWS and Azure. The latest version as of September 2016 is 16.04.1.

Kubuntu

The normal Ubuntu interface is based on a software called Unity. However, Kubuntu is based on a software called KDE Plasma desktop. This gives a different look and feel to the Ubuntu software. Kubuntu has the same features and software availability as Ubuntu. The official site for Kubuntu is https://www.kubuntu.org/

LINUX MINT

This is also based of the Ubuntu operating system. It comes pre-built with a lot of applications for the modern user in the space of photos and multimedia. This operating system is completely based on the open source community.

The official site for Linux Mint is https://www.linuxmint.com/

UBUNTU - ENVIRONNENT

We need to ensure we have the right hardware specifications in order to have Ubuntu installed.

SYSTEM REQUIREMENTS

Ensure the following system requirements are met before proceeding with the installation.

Memory	2GB RAM (recommended)
Disk Space	25GB of free hard disk space
Processor	2 GHz dual core processor or better
Other requirements	An optional DVD drive or USB drive with the Installer media. An internet connection to download the optional updates.

DOWNLOADING UBUNTU

Step 1 — To download Ubuntu, go to the following url — https://www.ubuntu.com/download/desktop

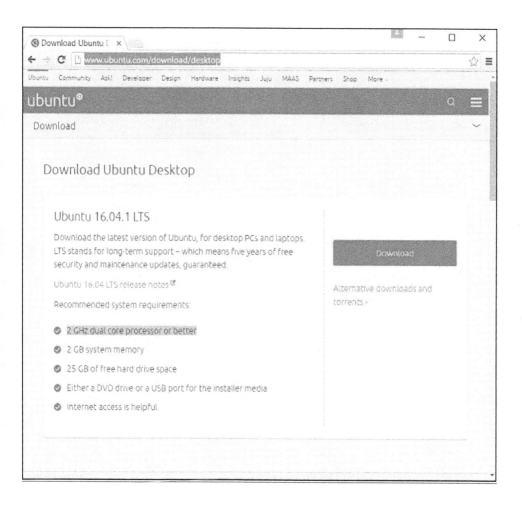

Step 2 — On this page, there is an option to download the older versions of Ubuntu if required. Click the Alternative downloads and torrents link.

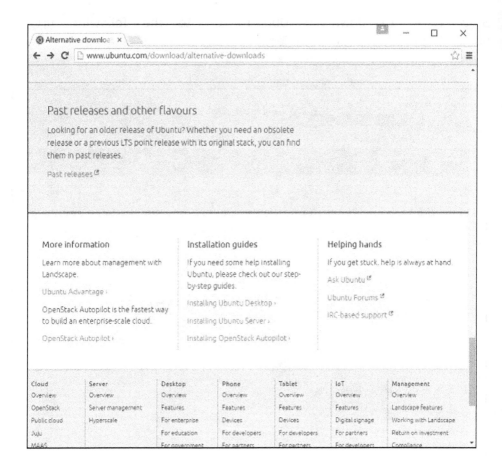

Step 3 — Go to Past releases link. It then presents a page with all the past releases of the Ubuntu software.

INSTALLING UBUNTU

Now let's learn about installing the desktop version of Ubuntu. For the purpose of this tutorial, we will go with the latest version which is 16.04. The installer is a ISO image which can be mounted on a DVD drive or USB stick. Once the image is booted on the machine, following are the steps for installation.

Step 1 − The first screen allows us to either install or try out Ubuntu. The try out option allows us to see the features of Ubuntu without actually installing it. However, we want to use Ubuntu, so let's choose the Install Ubuntu option.

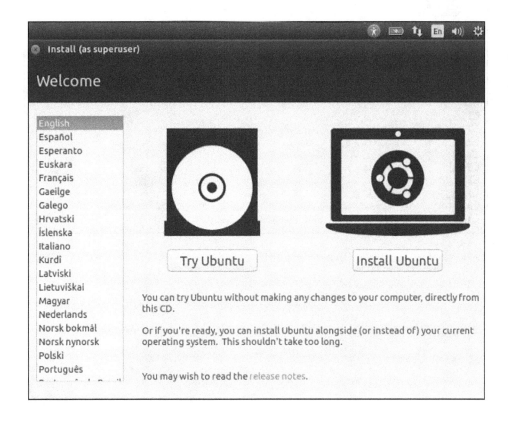

Step 2 — The next screen gives you 2 options. One is to download updates in the background while installing and the other is to install 3rd party software. Check the option to install 3rd party software. Then click the Continue button.

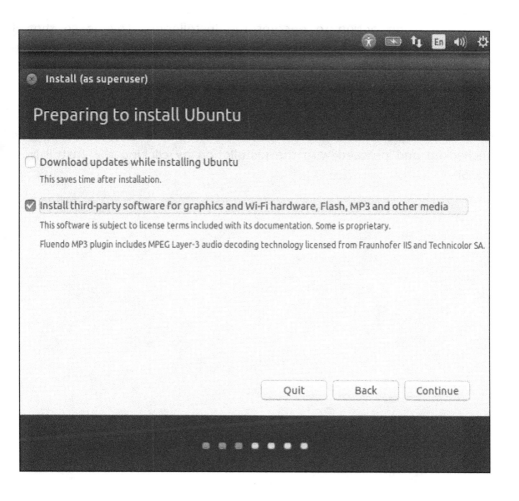

Step 3 – In the next screen, the following options are presented –

- The disk is erased and the installation is carried out. If there was another operating system already on the disk, then Ubuntu would detect it and give the user the option to install the operating system side by side.
- There is an option to encrypt the installation. This is so that if anybody else were to steal the data, they would not be able to decrypt the data.
- Finally, Linux offers a facility called LVM, which can be used for taking snapshots of the disk.

For the moment, to make the installation simple, let's keep the options unchecked and proceed with the installation by clicking the Install Now button.

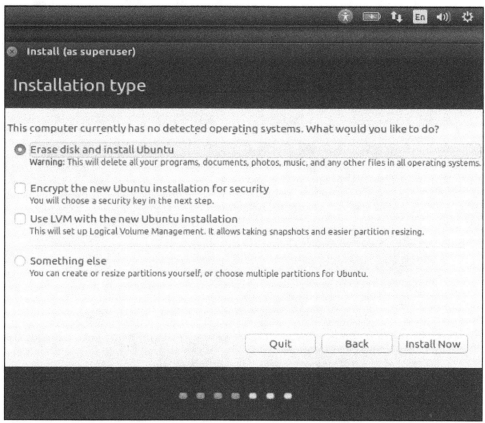

Step 4 – In the following screen, we will be prompted if we want to erase the disk. Click the Continue button to proceed.

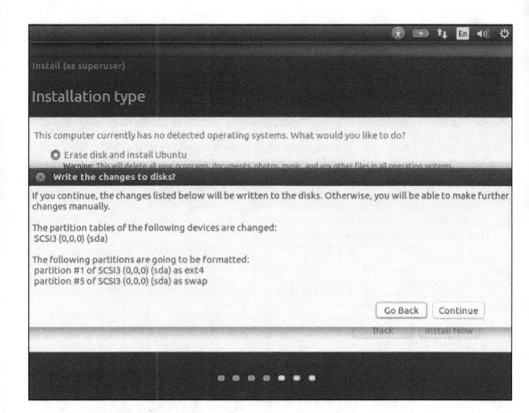

Step 5 – In this screen, we will be asked to confirm our location. Click the Continue button to proceed.

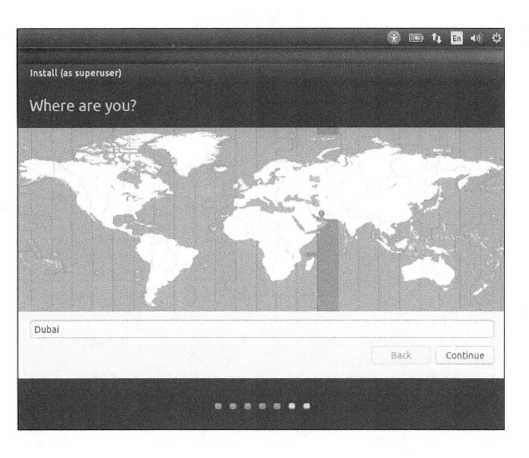

Step 6 — Now, we will be asked to confirm the language and the keyboard settings. Let us select English (UK) as the preferred settings.

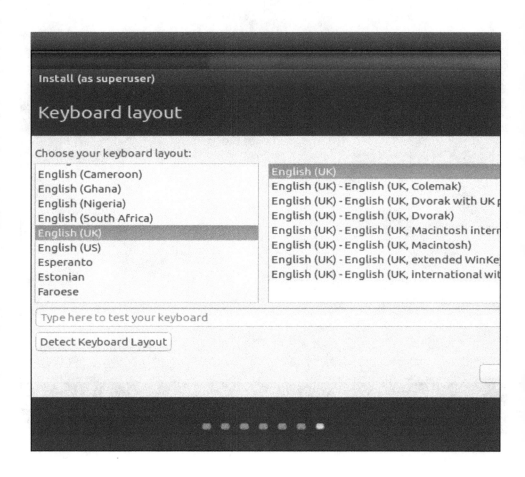

Step 7 — In the following screen, we will need to enter the user name, computer name and password which will be used to log into the system. Fill the necessary details as shown in the following screenshot. Then, click the continue button to proceed.

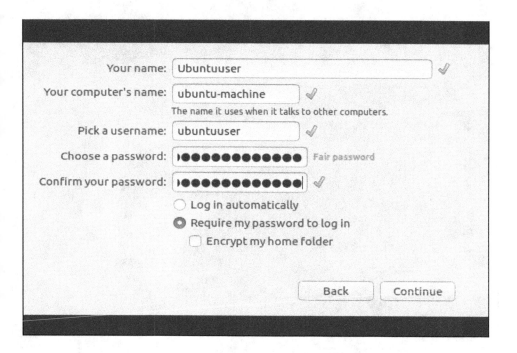

The system will now proceed with the installation and we will see the progress of the installation as shown in the following screenshot.

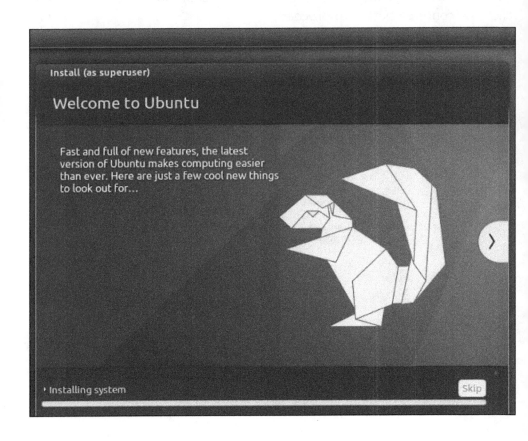

At the end of the installation, the system will prompt for a restart.

Step 8 – Click the Restart Now to proceed.

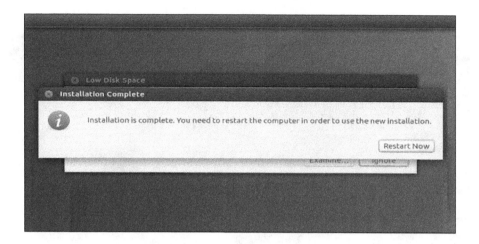

Once the restart is complete, log in with the username and password.

Once logged in, the desktop is presented as shown in the following screenshot.

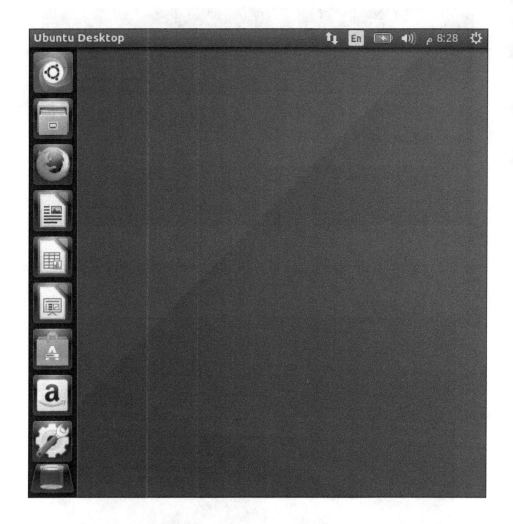

We now have a fully functional version of Ubuntu. In the subsequent chapters, we will look at the various features available.

Let us take a quick look at the Ubuntu environment before we proceed ahead with the remaining chapters.

The Control Panel

The Control Panel on the left-hand side of the screen presents shortcuts for all of the most used applications. Using these options, we can launch the LibreOffice component, the Firefox browser, the Software Center and many other applications.

The Menu Bar

When we launch any application, we will get the associated menu bar at the top of the application, which will have the different menu options for that application. We can choose to close the entire window or resize the window, if required.

TASKBAR

On the right-hand side of the screen is the task bar. The taskbar allows us to choose the change in volume settings, view the status of your internet connect, change your language and other settings, and view the battery status while working on a laptop.

Ubuntu - Device Drivers

By default, Ubuntu comes with pre-built required drivers for the mouse, keyboard, audio and video drivers. Long gone are the days where device drivers used to be a nightmare for Linux-based operating systems.

To view the options for devices, go to the settings options on the left-hand side control panel.

In the hardware section, you will see the various options for the hardware devices such as the display monitor, keyboard, mouse, etc.

For example, using the Display section, we can change the resolution of the screen along with other display settings as shown in the following screenshot.

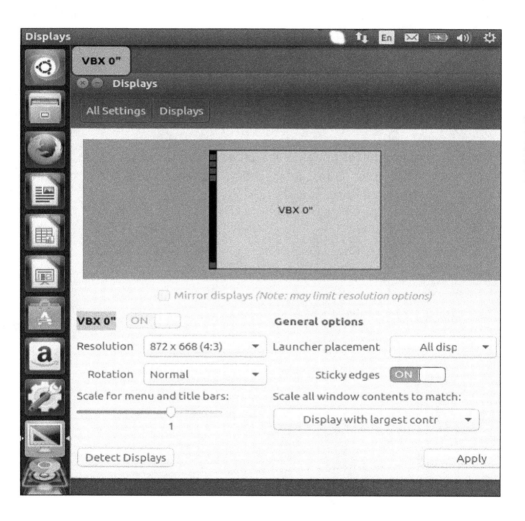

To install any additional drivers, we need to go to the respective driver website and download the necessary distribution for the particular device driver. Then, use the Software Center to install the required device driver.

Ubuntu - Software Center

Ubuntu has a Software Center using which you can install a host of applications. The Software Center is designed to search the Internet for available software which can be downloaded and installed.

Insalling Software

Step 1 — In the control panel, the Software Center appears on the left-hand side of the screen. In the following screenshot, it is encircled in a red box. Double-click to open it.

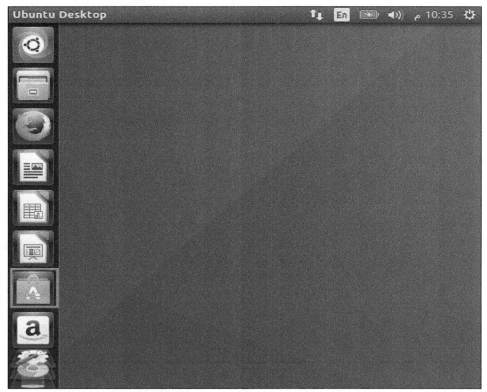

Once open, it shows the following options –

- View all the available software.
- All software currently installed on the machine.
- Any updates available for the software currently installed on the machine.

Step 2 – We can also browse through various software categories. For example, let's click the Audio category. We can see a list of available software for installation. As seen in the following screenshot, the application 'Rhythmbox' has already been installed.

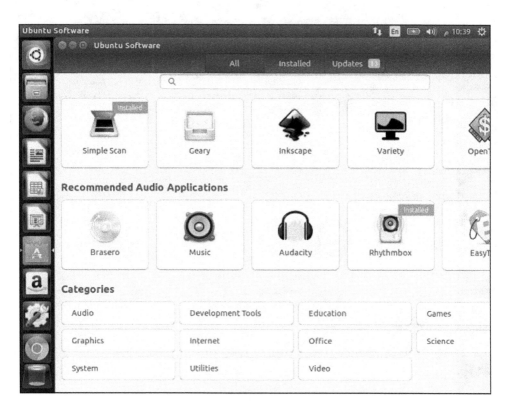

Step 3 – Now let us choose an application, say the Music application and
see how it installs.

Step 4 – Once we click the Music application, the following screenshot pops up. Click the Install button to begin the installation.

We will then see the Installing progress bar to show that the Music application is being installed.

Step 5 – Once the installation is complete, click the Launch button to launch the software.

REMOVING SOFTWARE

To see the list of already installed software on the machine, go to the Installed section of the Software Center application. This presents an option to remove the unwanted software if required, as shown in the following screenshot.

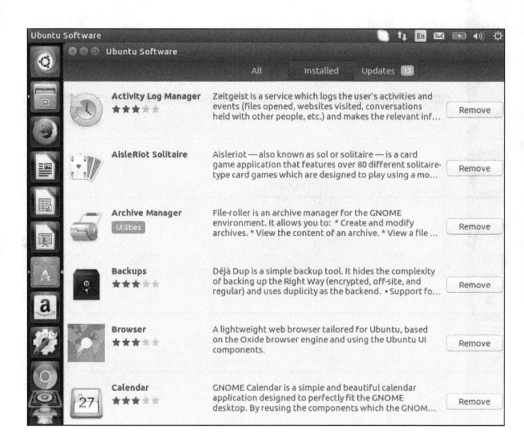

To remove any unwanted software, click the Remove button associated with the required software.

UPDATES

In the updates section, we can install critical updates available for the Ubuntu operating system. This section also shows the updates available for the software already installed on the system.

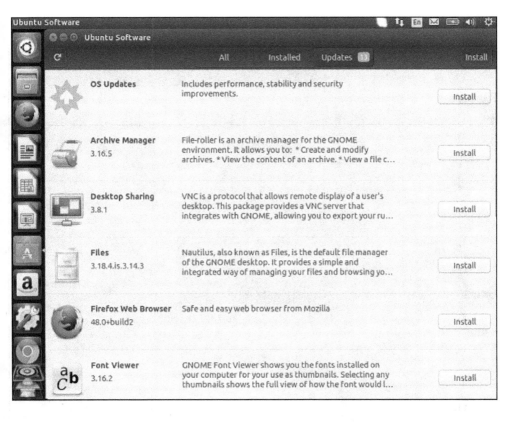

Click the Install button next to the desired update that needs to be installed.

Ubuntu - Browsers

The default browser for Ubuntu is Firefox and the latest version of Ubuntu always comes with the latest version of Firefox. On the desktop, you will see Firefox as the third component on the lefthand side. Double-click the icon to get started.

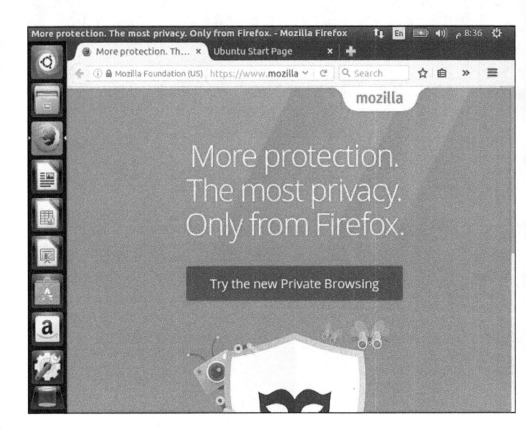

BROWSING SITES

We can type the address of the site we wish to visit in the address bar and hit enter to get the site loaded. We will get the same user-like experience as in Windows.

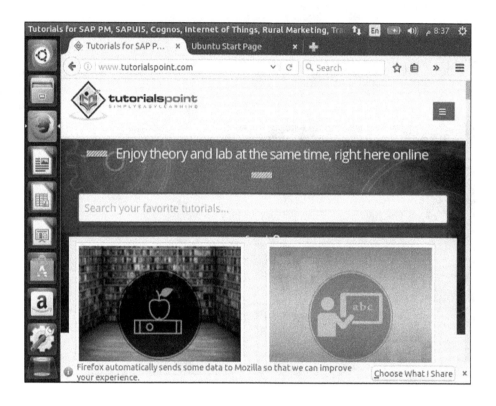

Installing Add-ons

Step 1 — Additional add-ons can be installed by going to the options and choosing the Add-ons option.

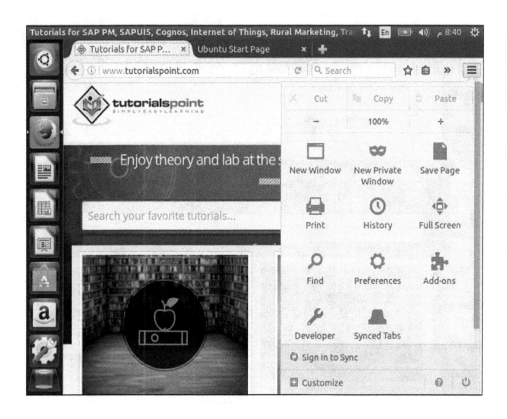

Using this option, we can view the add-ons installed and install new ones.

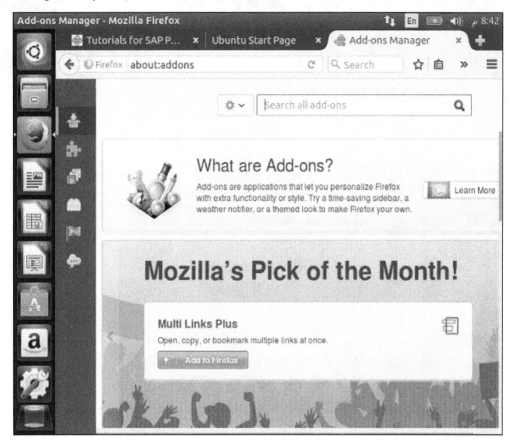

We can search for an add-on and then click the Install button to install an add-on.

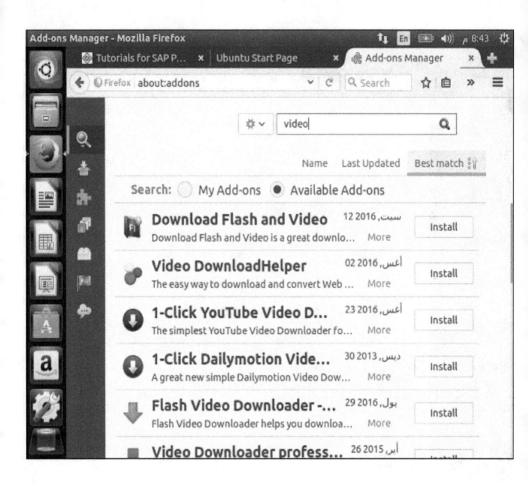

Step 2 – For example, let us install the "Download flash and Video" add-on as shown in the above screenshot. Click the Install button at its side.

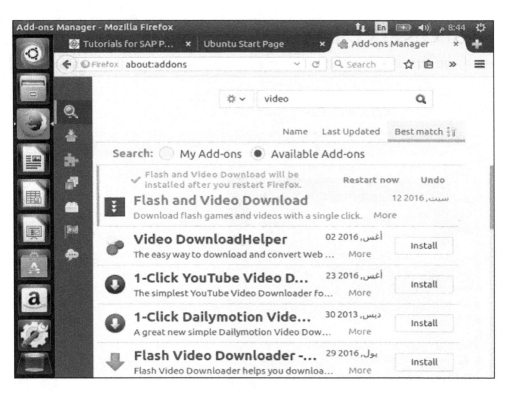

Step 3 — Once done, the browser will prompt for restart. After restarting the browser, go to the Installed Add-ons section. It will show the "Flash and Video Download" add-on installed as seen in the following screenshot.

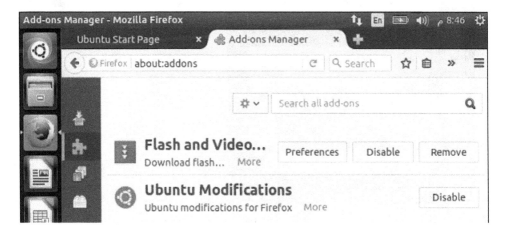

RESPONSIVE LAYOUT

Here, we can see how the browser will adapt to various screen sizes.

Step 1 − Click Options → Developer.

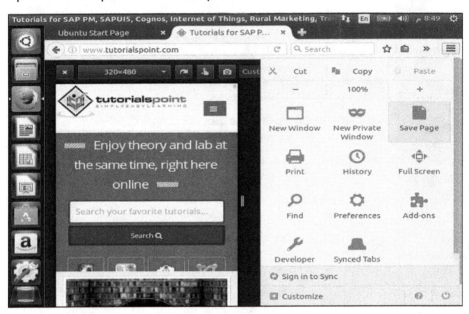

Step 2 − Click Responsive Design View.

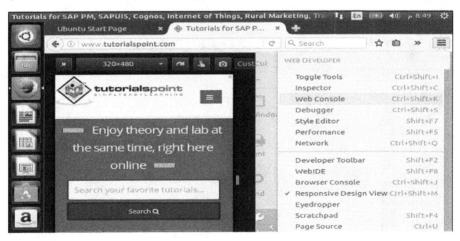

Now, we can view the site in different browser sizes to see if they would respond as they should if they are viewed on different devices.

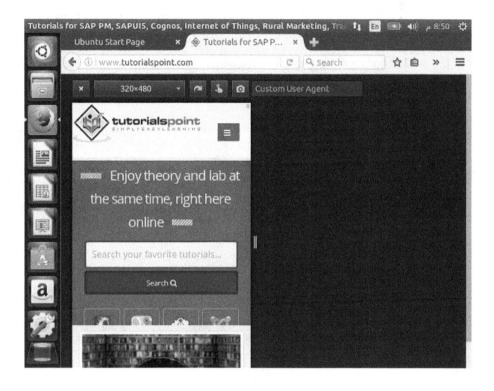

Using Chromium

The default application for Chrome usage on Ubuntu is called Chromium. Following are the steps to install Chromium –

Step 1 – Go to the application manager for Ubuntu and go to the Internet section.

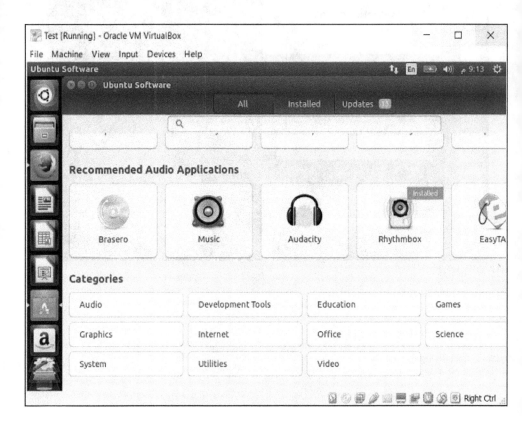

Step 2 − In the following screen, click the Chromium web browser option.

Step 3 – Next, click the Install button to install Chromium.

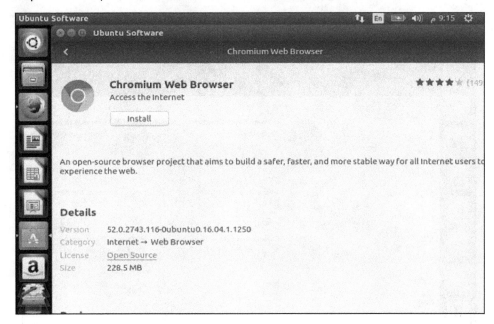

Step 4 – Once the browser is installed, the chromium browser option will appear on the left-hand panel. Use it to launch Chromium.

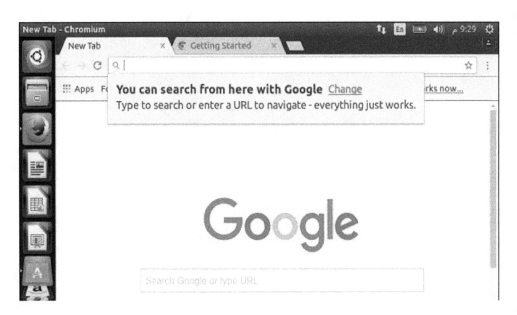

UBUNTU - EMAIL

The default email client in Ubuntu is Thunderbird. The following steps show how to start using Thunderbird as the email client software.

We can quickly search for any application using the Search facility in Ubuntu.

Step 1 — Double-click on the search facility, enter the keyword of email and the search result of Thunderbird email will appear.

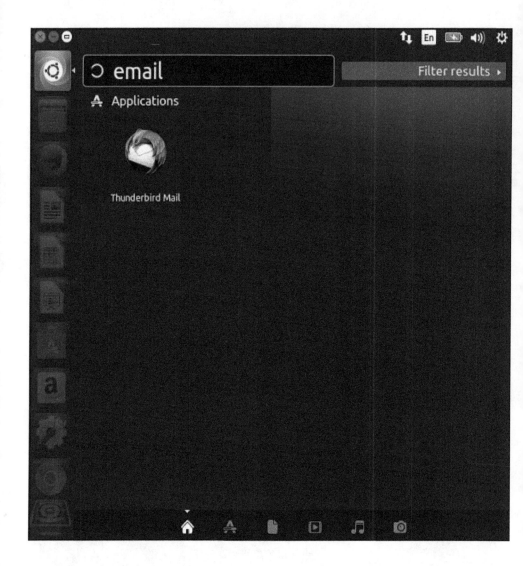

Step 2 – Double-click the search result to launch the Thunderbird mail client. Once the email client is launched, there will be a request to link an email account to the mail client.

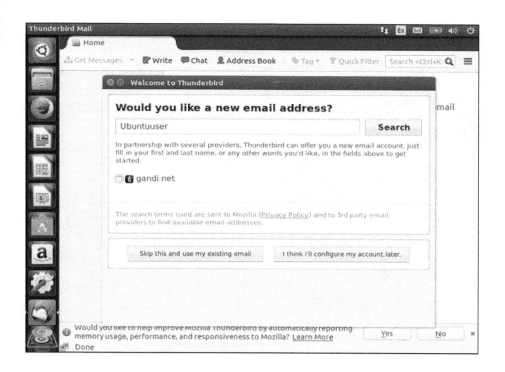

Step 3 – Click "Skip this and use my existing email" button, so that we can use the current email credentials.

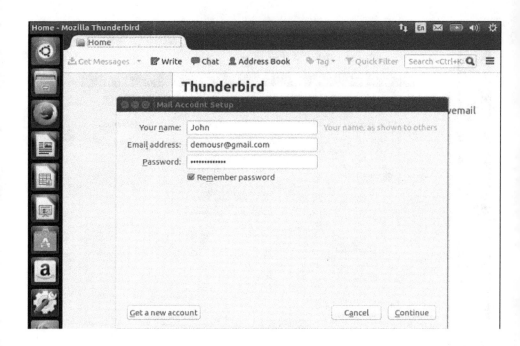

Step 4 — Enter the required credentials and click the Continue button to proceed. Once configured, the email client will then provide the common features for any email client. Now, we will be able to view the Inbox as well as all the messages in the Inbox.

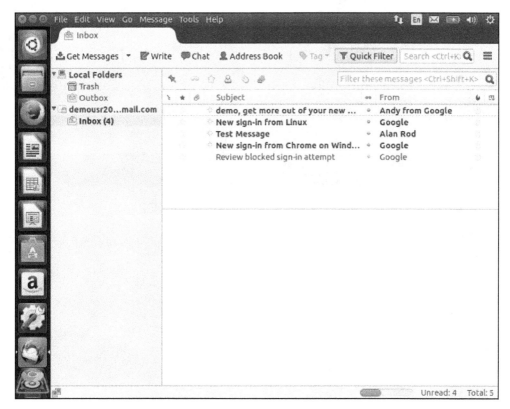

Step 5 – Click any message to get more information on the received email as shown in the following screenshot.

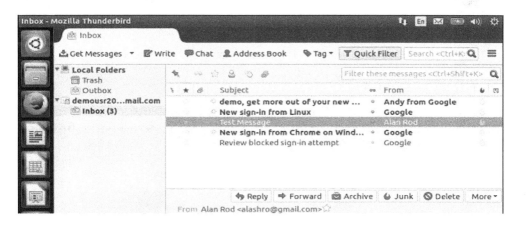

SENDING EMAIL

Step 1 — In the Menu option, click the Write option to create a message which needs to be sent.

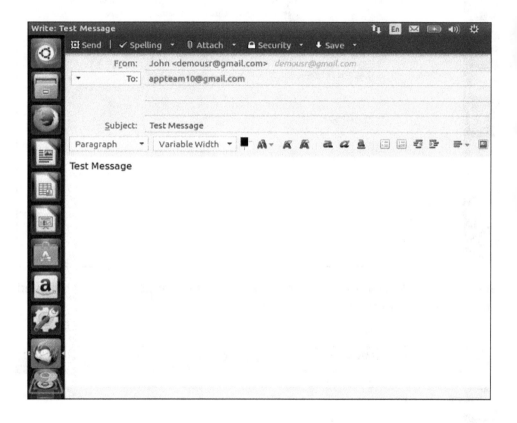

Step 2 — Enter the message details. Once complete, click the Send Button. Note, there is also an option to spell check and add attachments.

The sent messages will be displayed in the Sent messages section as shown in the following screenshot.

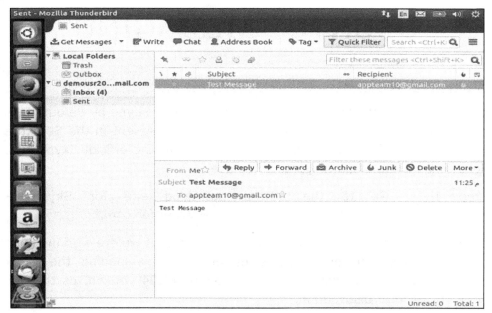

On the right-hand side of the screen, there are shortcuts available to view mail, compose a new message, and view contacts as seen in the following screenshot.

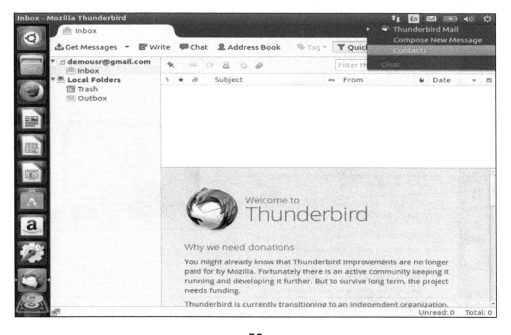

UBUNTU - MESSAGING

The default messaging software used on desktops today is the Skype software. This software is distributed by Microsoft. Skype by default does not come with Ubuntu installation. It will not be present in the Software Center. We have to download and install it from the official Skype site. Following are the steps to get this in place.

Step 1 – Go to the official download site for Skype – https://www.skype.com/en/downloadskype/skype-for-computer/

Step 2 – The site will automatically understand that we are working from a Linux distribution and provide options for downloading the Linux version of Skype. We will choose the Ubuntu 12.04 version, as this will work on the later distribution.

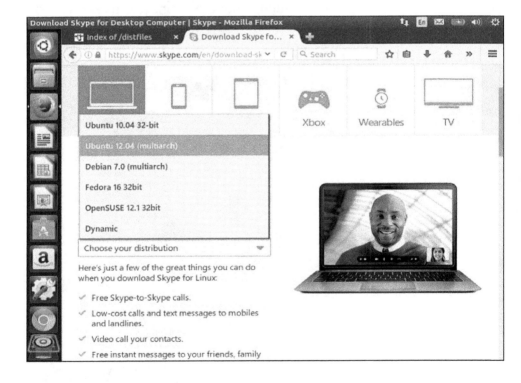

Step 3 — Once the package is downloaded, it will open in the Software Center. Choose the Install option to install the package.

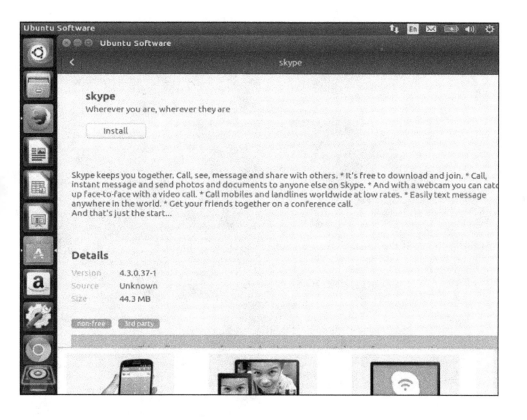

Step 4 – Once Skype is installed, we can search for it and launch it accordingly.

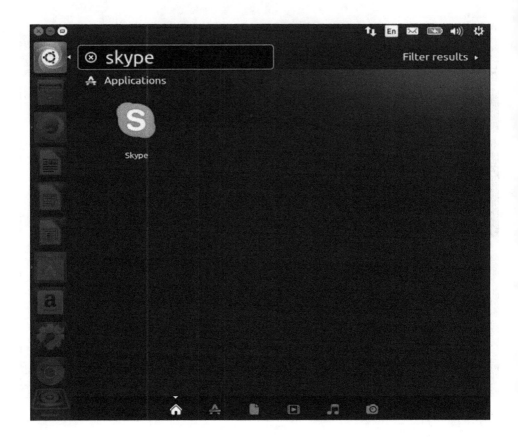

Step 5 — Click the 'I Agree' button in the following screenshot.

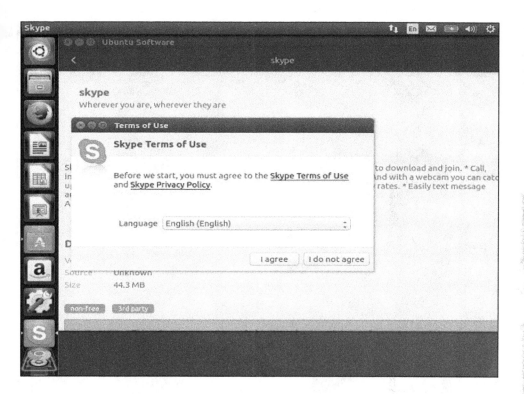

Skype will now launch.

Step 6 – Enter the required credentials to start using Skype.

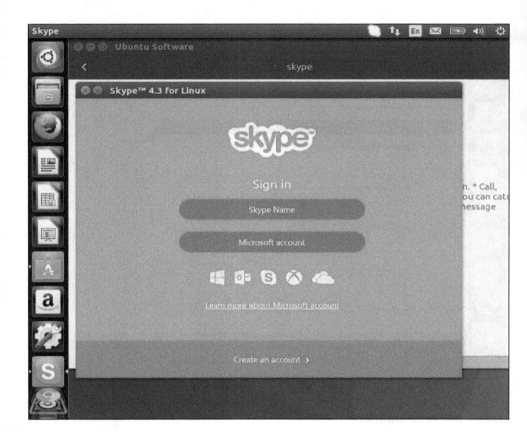

Ubuntu - Media Players

Ubuntu provides some options when it comes to Media Players.

Rhythmbox

By default, it contains a music player called Rhythmbox.

We can search for it, and launch it as shown in the following screenshot.

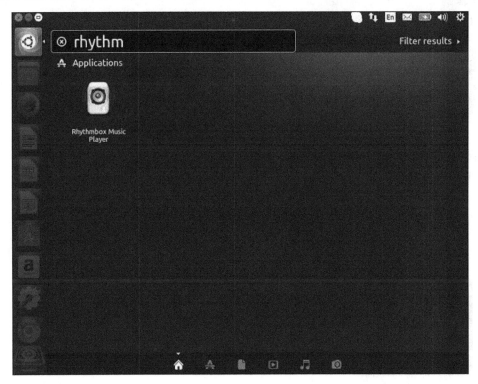

The general user interface of Rhythmbox is as shown in the following screenshot. It can be used to play music from the computer or even download and listen to songs from the Internet.

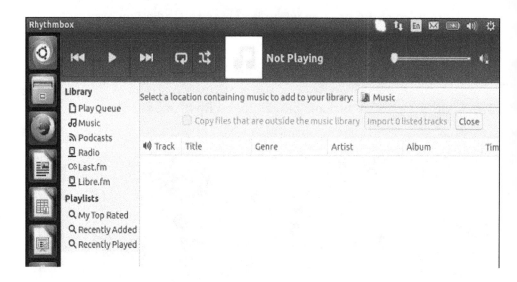

To add music, click the File menu option and choose the Add Music option.

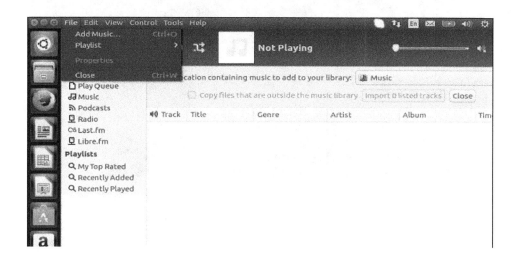

To listen to radio stations, click on the Radio option on the left hand side of the screen, click the desired radio station, and click the play button.

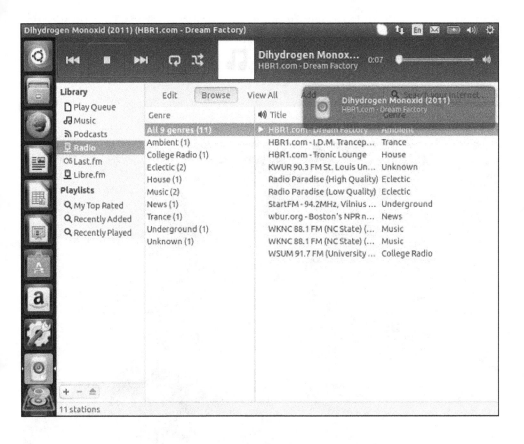

SHOTWELL

Shotwell is the default application for managing photos. This application does a good job in offering the users all the possible options required for managing photos and photo albums.

We can search for the application and launch it as shown in the following screenshot.

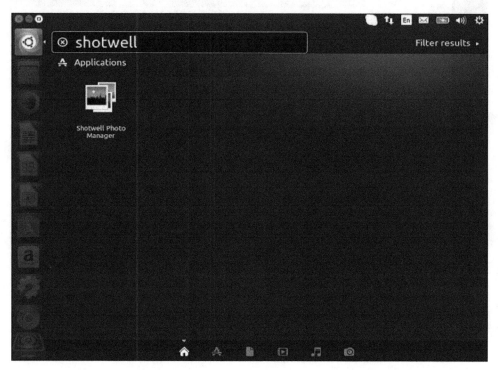

The general user interface of the application is as shown in the following screenshot.

To import the existing folders, choose the menu option of File → Import from folder.

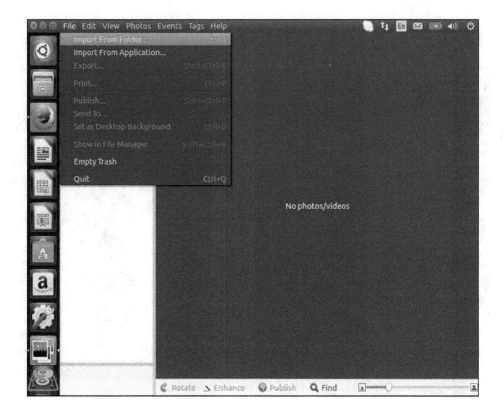

Then choose the location to which the photos are to be imported and click the OK button.

It now gives an option to either copy the photos from the place or to Import in place. Let's choose the option to copy the photos.

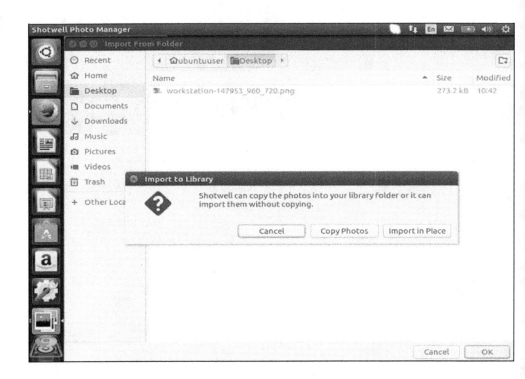

Once done, the photos will then be visible in the source location.

Enhancement tools can be used to enhance the picture. To do so, just click the picture and choose the Enhance option from the left-hand context menu.

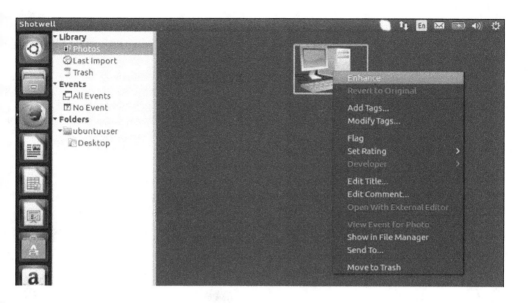

We can then enlarge the picture, auto correct it, remove red-eye along with many other adjustment features.

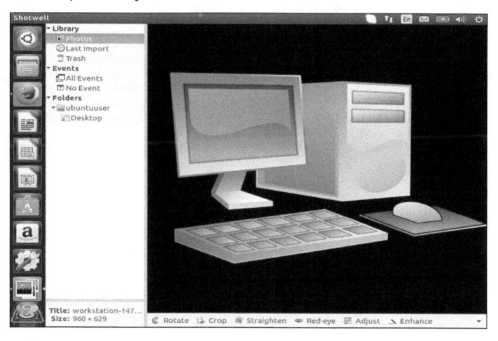

VLC

VLC is the most widely used video player and this is also available in Ubuntu.

To get VLC installed, following are the steps.

Step 1 – Go to the Software Center and choose the Video option.

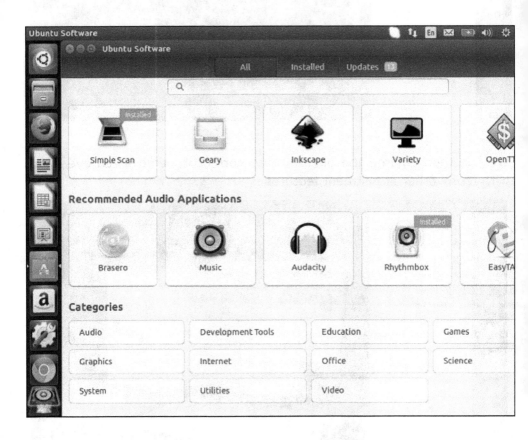

Step 2 – Choose the option of VLC media player as shown in the following screenshot.

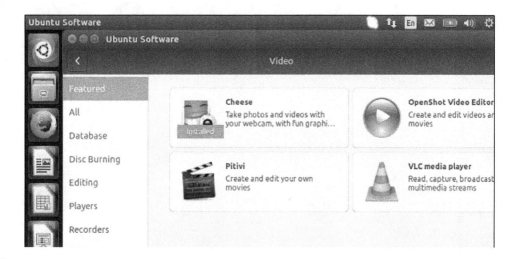

Step 3 – Click the Install button in the following screen to begin the installation of VLC media player.

Step 4 — Once complete, click the Launch button.

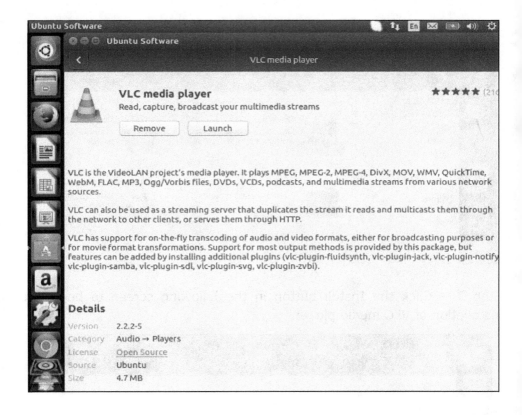

VLC media player will now launch. The media player can be normally used as on a Windows machine.

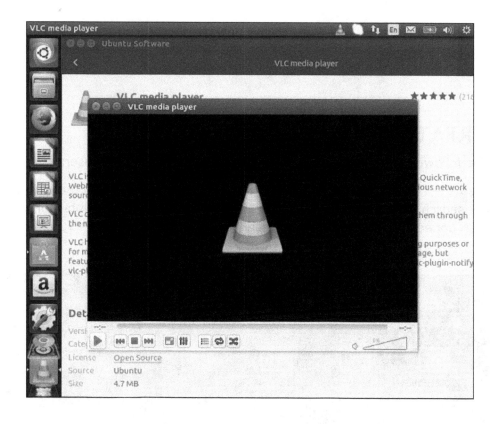

UBUNTU - USER MANAGEMENT

Ubuntu provides the facility to create new users who can be authorized to log on to the system. Let's look at the different functions that can be performed with the help of user management.

CREATING USERS

The following steps need to be performed for the creation of users.

Step 1 — Launch the user management console from the search menu. In the search menu, enter the keyword of users. The User Accounts icon will then appear. Double-click on the User Accounts icon.

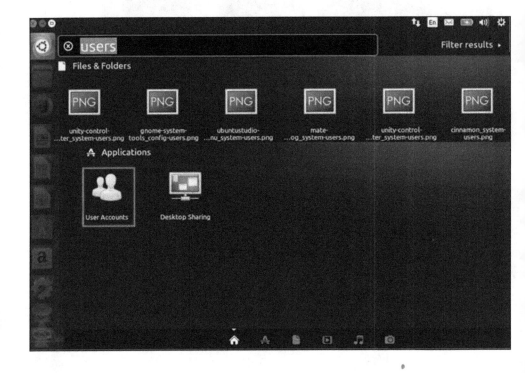

Step 2 − The user management screen will then pop up as shown in the following screenshot. To perform any sort of user management, we first need to press the Unlock button and enter our administrator credentials.

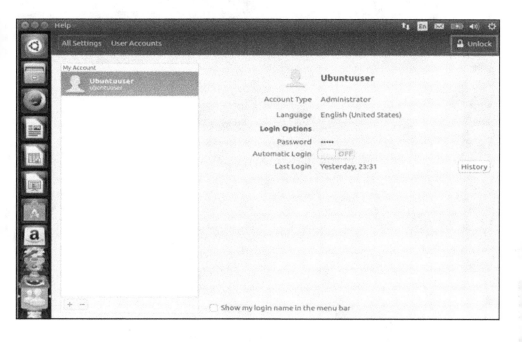

Step 3 — Enter the administrator credentials in the pop-up box which comes up and click the Authenticate button.

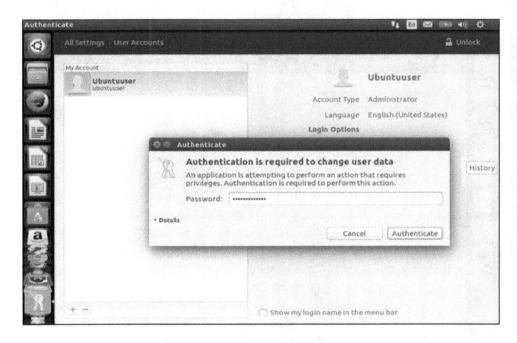

Once we click Authenticate, all the user management functions on the screen will become enabled.

Step 4 – Click the plus button to create a user.

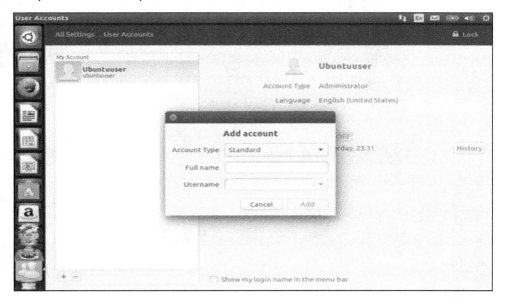

Step 5 – Enter the user details. We can only create Standard and Administrator account types.

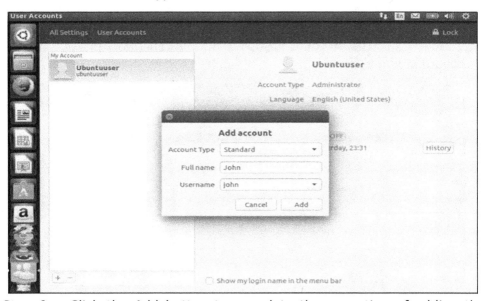

Step 6 – Click the Add button to complete the operation of adding the user.

Enabling the User Account

When the user is created, the user account is disabled. This is because a password has not been associated with the account.

Following are the steps to enable the user account.

Step 1 – Click the Account disabled option. This will prompt for the password dialog box.

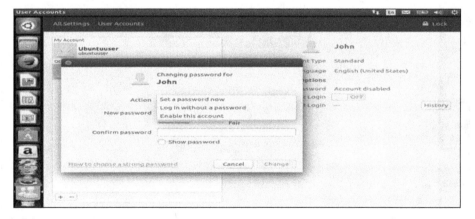

We have the option to either set a password, log in without a password, or enable the account. A good practice is to always set a password for an account.

Step 2 – To set the password and click the Change button.

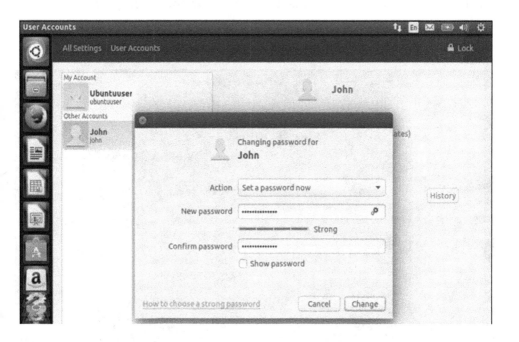

Step 3 – The account will now be enabled. Log in using the newly created account.

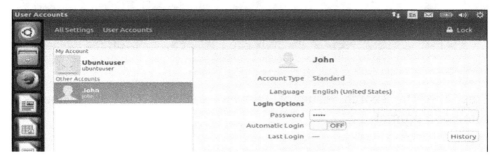

Managing User Permissions and Groups

To manage user permissions and groups, an additional package needs to be installed. Following are the steps to manage user permissions and groups.

Step 1 – Go to the search option and type the command keyword.

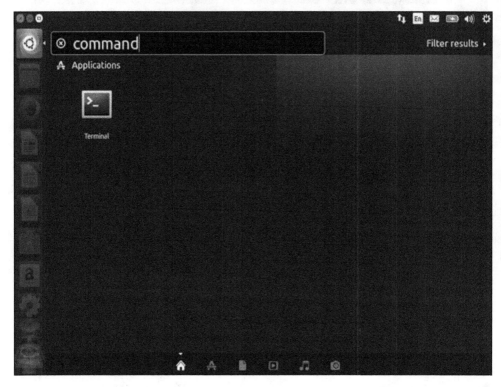

Step 2 – The search result of Terminal appears. Click it to open the command prompt.

Step 3 – Next, issue the following command.

sudo apt-get install gnome-system-tools

The apt-get command line is used to install additional packages from the Internet for the Ubuntu system. Here, we are telling Ubuntu that we want to install additional system tools so that we can manage user permissions and groups.

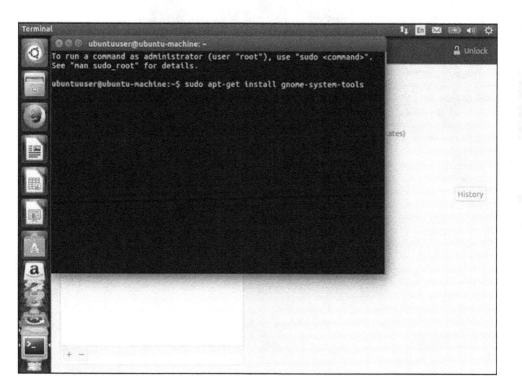

Step 4 – We will then be prompted for the password of the current logged in account and to also confirm to download the necessary packages for the installation. Enter the 'Y' option to proceed.

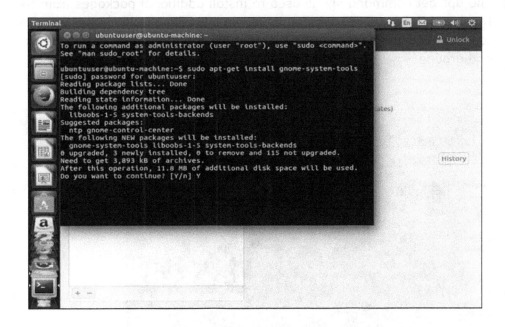

Step 5 – Once the installation is complete, when we search for users in the search option in Ubuntu, we can see an additional option of Users and Groups.

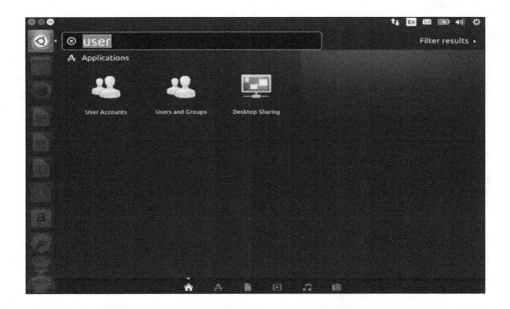

Step 6 – Click the Users and Groups option. Now, there will be an additional option of user and groups.

Step 7 – Click the Advanced settings button. We will be prompted to enter the password of the current logged on user to authenticate. Enter the password and click the Authenticate button.

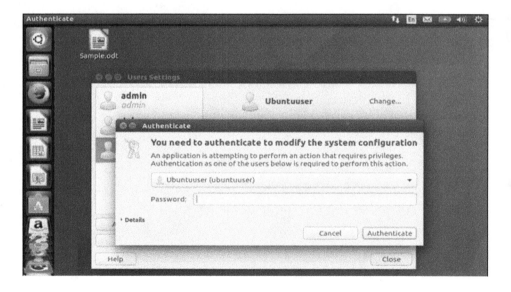

Step 8 – In the next dialog box which appears, we will then be able to assign the required user privileges to the user.

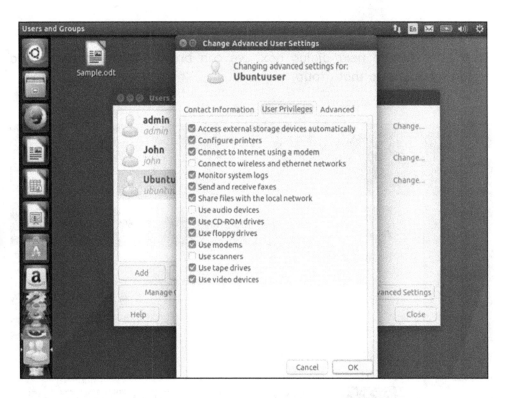

Step 9 — Now, if we click on the Groups option, we will see that it has the option to create and delete groups.

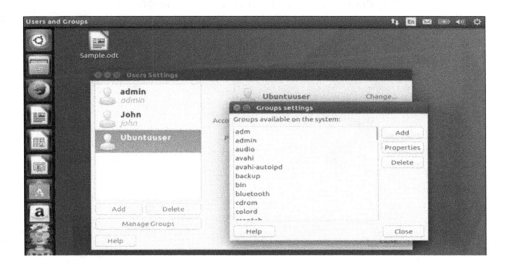

Step 10 − Click on the Add button to add a group.

Step 11 − In the next dialog box, we can provide a group name and assign members to that group.

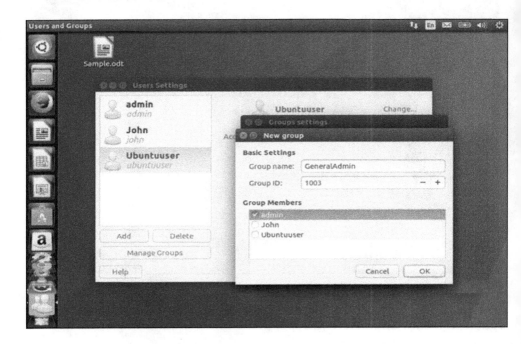

Step 12 − Finally, click the OK button to create the group.

Ubuntu - Files and Folders

To open the file like explorer in Ubuntu, click the Files option in the software launcher. In the following screenshot the Files icon is encircled in red.

On clicking the icon, the following screen which is the File like explorer in Ubuntu opens up.

CREATING A FOLDER

Step 1 – To create a folder, choose a location where the folder needs to be created.

Step 2 – Then right-click and choose the option of New Folder.

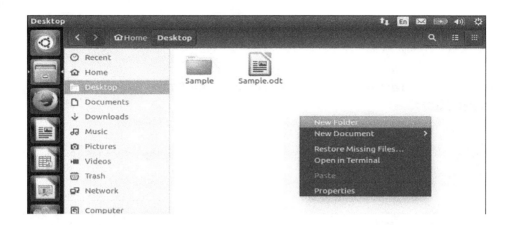

Step 3 – Provide a name for the folder accordingly.

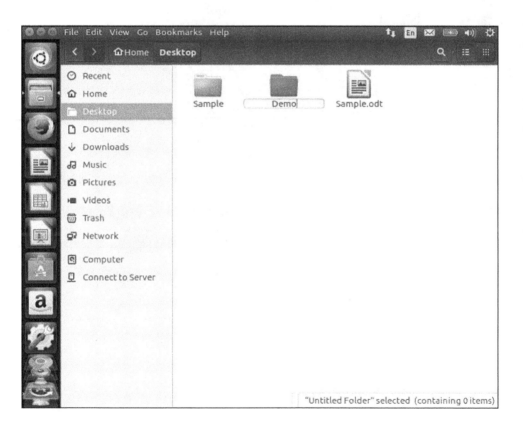

Renaming a Folder

Step 1 – To rename a folder, right-click the folder which needs to be renamed.

Step 2 – Right-click and choose the rename option from the context menu.

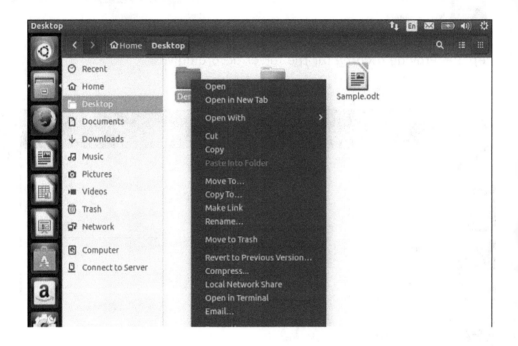

Step 3 – Provide the new name of the folder accordingly.

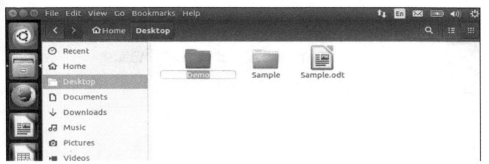

Note — There are other options such as move or copy the folder or move the folder to trash.

SEEING THE PROPERTIES OF A FILE

To see the properties of a file, right-click the file and choose the Properties option from the context menu.

Using the option, we can view the properties of the file and modify the permissions of the file accordingly as shown in the following screenshot.

UBUNTU - WORD WRITER

The Word Writer comes in-built in Ubuntu and is available in the Software launcher.

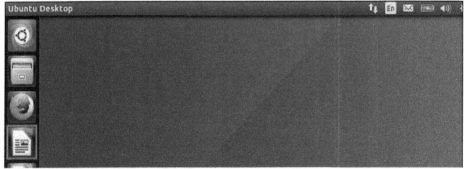

The icon is encircled in red in the above screenshot. Once we click on the icon, the writer will launch.

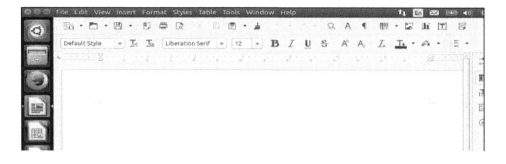

We can start typing in the Writer as we normally would do in Microsoft Word.

SAVING DOCUMENTS

To save a document, just click on the save menu option as shown in the following screenshot.

Specify the location, the name of the file and then click the Save button.

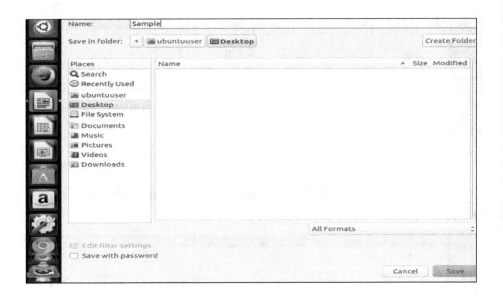

CREATING NEW DOCUMENTS

To create a new document, choose the new menu option as shown in the following screenshot. It shows an option to create various types of documents.

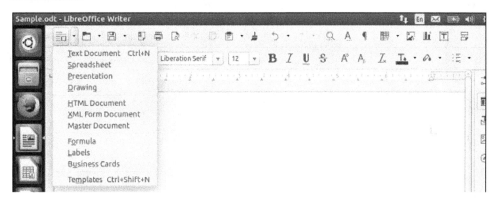

OPENING AN EXISTING DOCUMENT

To open an existing document, choose the option of opening an existing document from the file menu options as shown in the following screenshot. The option icon is encircled in red.

Once the open menu option is clicked, it presents a dialog box with an option to choose the file which needs to be opened. Click on the desired file and then click Open.

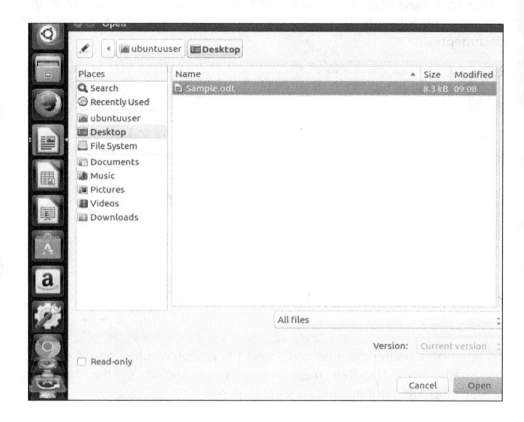

WORKING WITH TABLES

Tables can be inserted using the Insert table option as shown in the following screenshot.

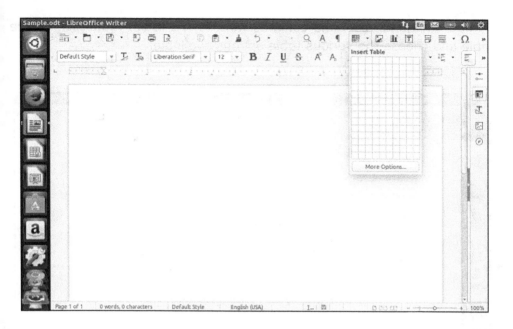

Once the table has been added, we can then work on the table as we would on Microsoft Word.

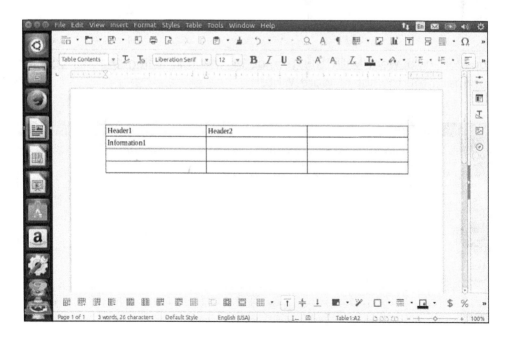

To add additional rows and columns work to the table, right-click on the table and choose the various table options available.

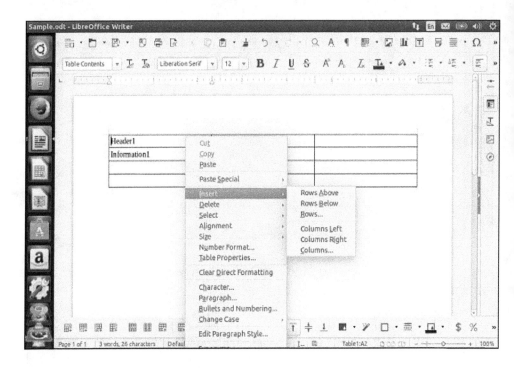

You can also work with the format of the text using the various font options in the toolbar of Word Writer.

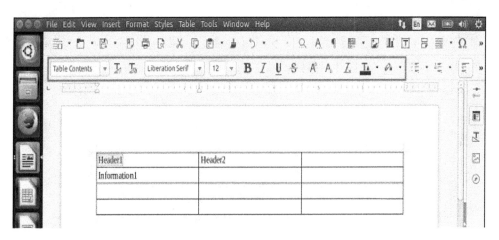

UBUNTU - SPREADSHEETS

The default application for spreadsheets in Ubuntu is called Calc. This is also available in the software launcher.

Once we click on the icon, the spreadsheet application will launch.

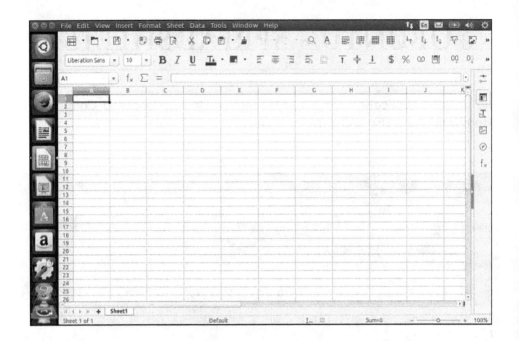

We can edit the cells as we would normally do in a Microsoft Excel application.

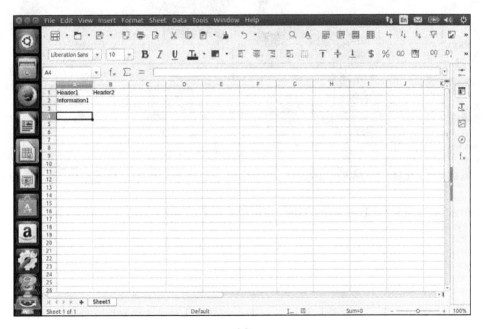

98

ADDING FORMULAS

Formulas can be added in the same manner as in Microsoft Excel. The following example shows an excel sheet which has 3 columns. The 3rd column is the multiplication of the Units and Unit price column.

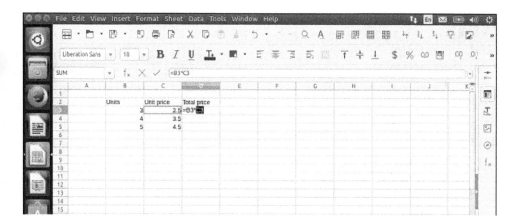

The columns can be dragged to ensure the same formula is repeated for each row.

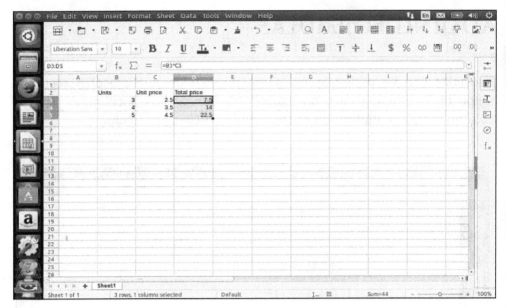

SAVING A SHEET

To save a sheet, go to the Save As menu option as shown in the following screenshot.

Provide the name, location of the spreadsheet and click the Save button to save the sheet.

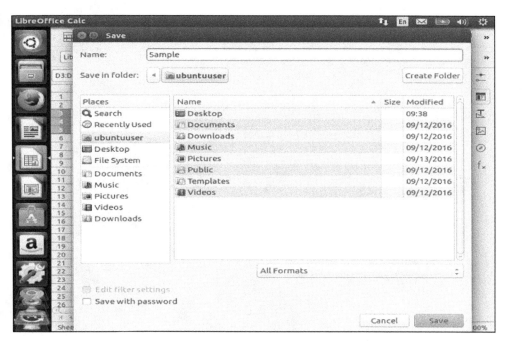

There are various other formatting options available in the toolbar in the Calc application as shown in the following screenshot.

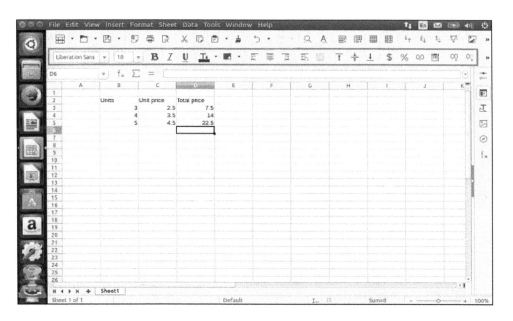

Inserting Charts

On the right-hand side of the Calc application, there are various other options. One of them is to insert a chart in the spreadsheet.

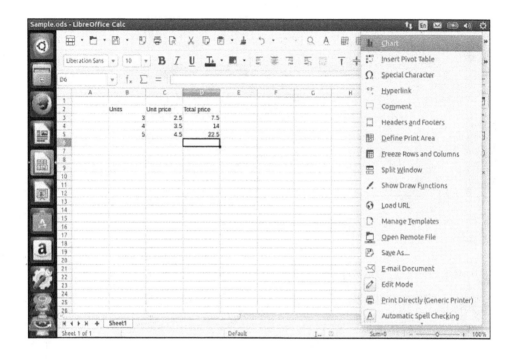

Once we click the Chart option, it will prompt for the type of Chart to be inserted. Choose a chart type and click the Finish button.

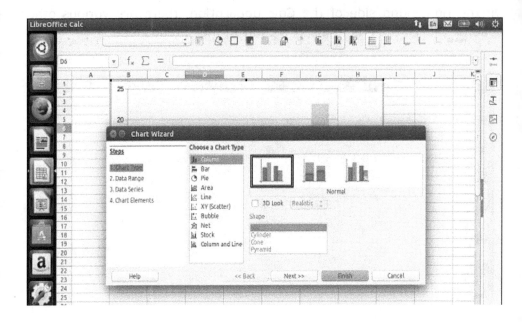

Now, we can see the Chart in the spreadsheet.

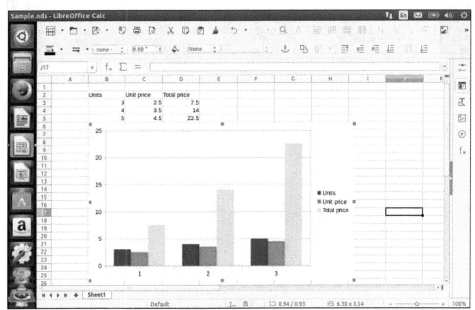

UBUNTU - LIBREOFFICE

LibreOffice is a suite of office products available in Ubuntu. It is similar to the Microsoft suite of products although there are some features of Microsoft Office that does not work with LibreOffice and vice versa.

LibreOffice was first introduced in the year 1985 by a company called StarOffice. In the year 2002, the suite was taken by OpenOffice.org with Sun Microsystems being a major contributor to the product. From the year 2010 onwards, a separate branch of the source code of the product was taken which is now known as LibreOffice.

We will look at the LibreOffice writer and Calc in subsequent chapters. In this chapter, we will look at LibreOffice Impress which is the PowerPoint version of Microsoft.

The LibreOffice suite comes in-built in Ubuntu and is available in the Software launcher.

The icon of LibreOffice is encircled in red in the above screenshot. Once we click on the icon, the Impress Software will launch and the following screen will pop up.

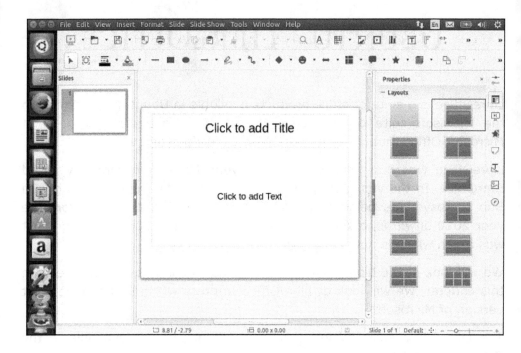

The interface looks quite similar to Microsoft PowerPoint. We can then modify the content on the slides as required.

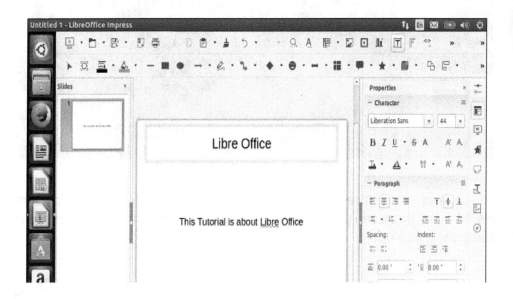

ADDING SLIDES

Adding slides to Impress is pretty similar to Microsoft PowerPoint. There are multiple ways of adding slides. One way is to use the Duplicate Slide option.

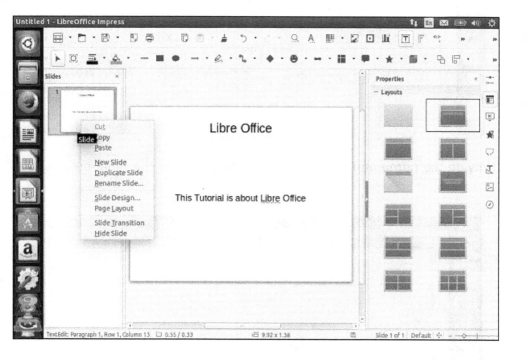

We can decide on the slide layout of the new slide by choosing the layout from the layout panel that appears on the right-hand side of the screen.

SAVING SLIDES

To save the presentation, choose the 'Save As' menu option.

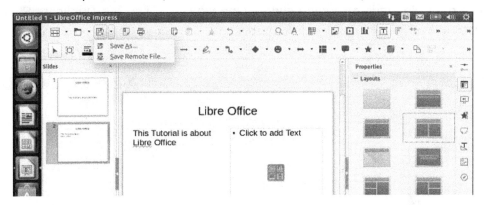

Provide the name and location of the slide and click the Save button.

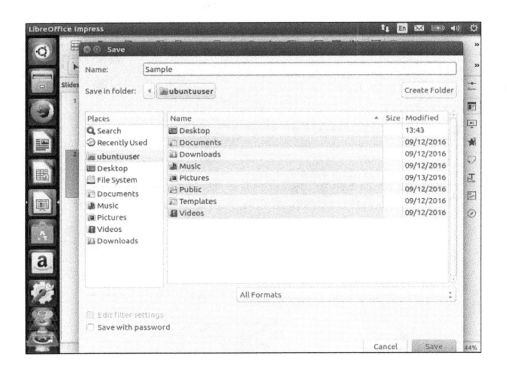

Opening Slides

To open an existing presentation, click the Open menu option.

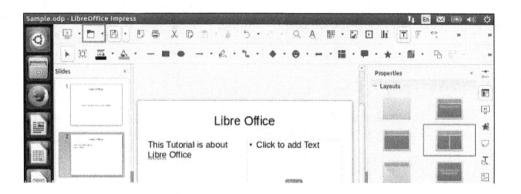

Choose the location and name of the file. Click the Open button to open the presentation.

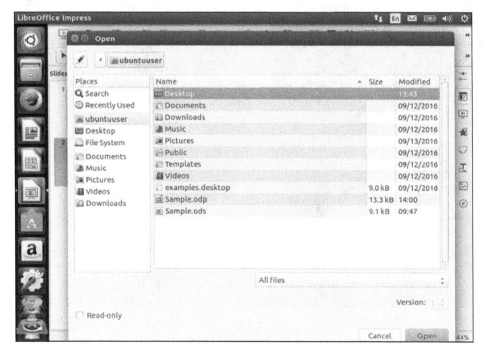

Ubuntu - Command Line

Ubuntu is a Linux based operating system and most Linux users are more familiar with the command line interface. In this chapter, we will go through some of the popular command line's used in Ubuntu.

Invoking the Command Line

To invoke the command line, go to the search option and enter the command keyword in the search box.

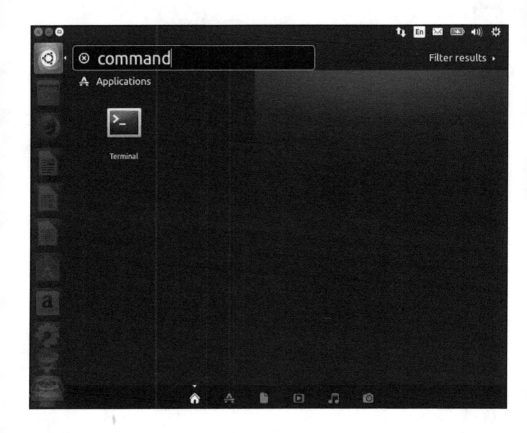

The search result will give the Terminal option. Double-lick to get the command line as shown in the following screenshot.

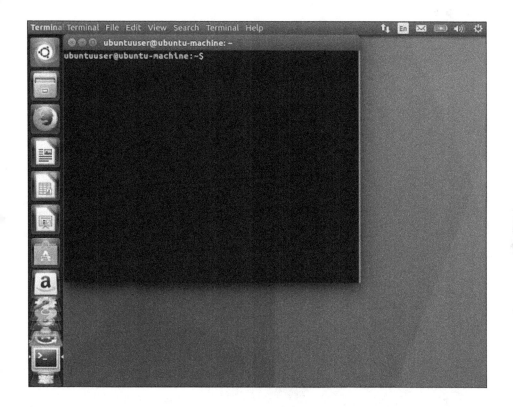

DIRECTORY LISTING

The easiest command to start with, is the directory listing command which is used to list the directory contents.

Syntax

ls –option directoryname

Parameters

- Option — These are the options to be specified with the ls command.
- Directoryname — This is the optional directory name that can be specified along with the ls command.

111

Output

The output will be the listing of the directory contents.

Example

In the following example, we just issue the ls command to list the directory contents.

The directory listing of the current directory will be shown as the output.

Another variant of the ls command is to list the directory, but with more details on each line item. This is shown in the following screenshot with the ls –l command.

CLEARING THE SCREEN

To clear the screen, we can use the clear command.

Syntax

clear

Parameters

None

Output

The command line screen will be cleared.

COMMAND HELP

To get more information on a command, we can use the 'man' command.

Syntax

man commandname

Parameters

Commandname – This is the name of the command for which more information is required.

Output

The information on the command will be displayed.

Example

Following is an example of the 'man' command. If we issue the 'man ls' command, we will get the following output. The output will contain information on the ls command.

Finding For Files

We can use the find command to find for files.

Syntax

find filepattern

Parameters

Filepattern – This is the pattern used to find for files.

Output

The files based on the file pattern will be displayed.

Example

In this example, we will issue the following command.

find Sample.*

This command will list all the files which start with the word 'Sample'.

WHOAMI

This command is used to display who is the current logged on user.

Syntax

whoami

Parameters

None

Output

The name of the current logged on user will be displayed.

Example

In this example, we will issue the following command.

Whoami

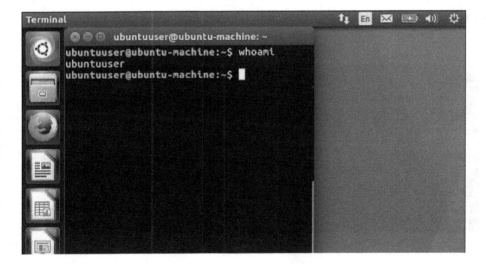

PRESENT WORKING DIRECTORY

This command will display the current working directory.

Syntax

pwd

Parameters

None

Output

The current working directory will be displayed.

Example

In this example, we will issue the following command.

Pwd

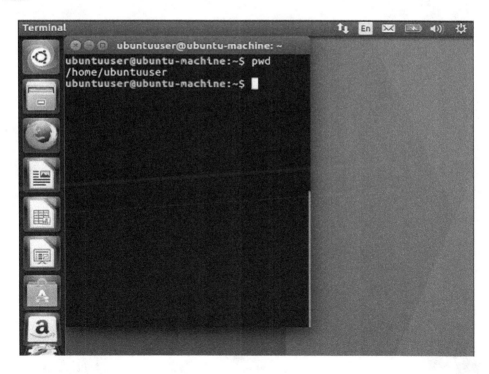

Ubuntu - Scripting

Since we have the ability to work with the command line which we covered in the previous chapter, it is common to create scripts which can perform simple jobs. Scripting is normally used to automate administrative tasks. Let's create a simple script using the following steps. The script will be used to display the IP address assigned to the machine.

Step 1 − Open the editor. Just like notepad in Windows, Ubuntu has a text editor. In the search dialog box, enter the keyword of editor. Then double-click on the Text Editor option.

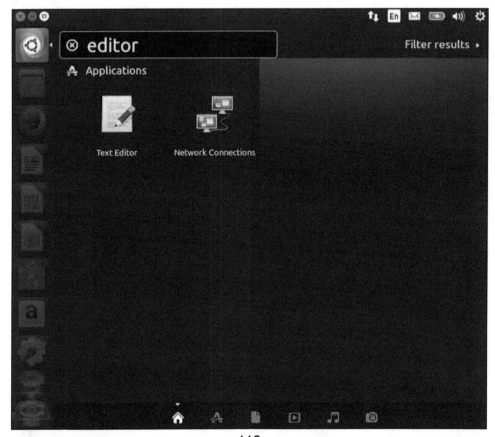

The following editor screen pops up.

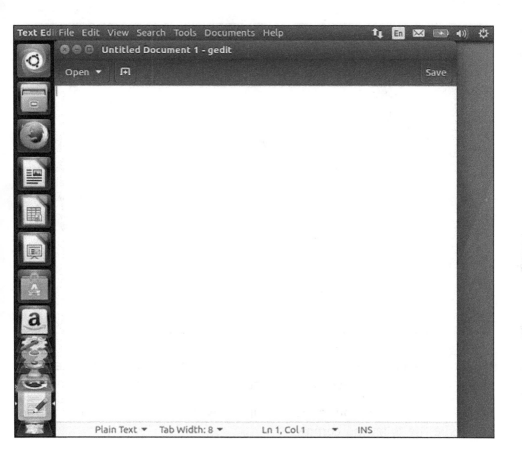

Step 2 — Enter the following text in the editor.

originalAddress=@(ifconfig | grep "inet addr" | head –n 1 | cut –d ":" –f 2 | cut –d
" " –f 1)

echo $originalAddress

Step 3 – Save the file as write-ip.sh.

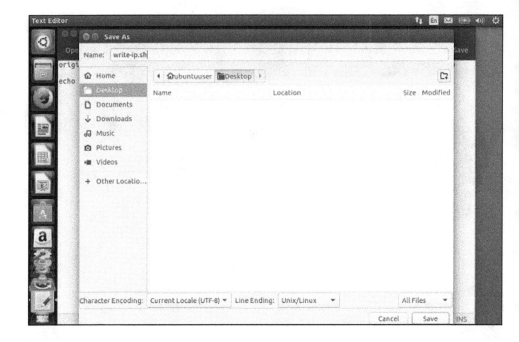

Now once you have saved the file, we need to assign the file some execute rights. Otherwise, we will not be able to execute the file.

Step 4 – Go to the command prompt, navigate to the Desktop location and issue the following command.

chmod a+x write-ip.sh

The above command will provide execute permissions to the file.

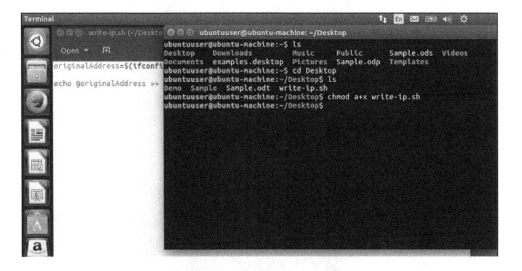

Step 5 – Now, we can execute the file by issuing the following command.

./write-ip.sh

The output will be the IP address assigned to the machine as shown in the following screenshot.

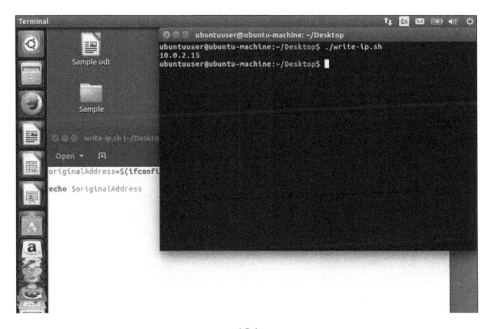

UBUNTU - NETWORKING

Ubuntu provides the options to view the network details of the workstation. Following are the steps to view the network details of the machine.

Step 1 − In the search dialog box, type the keyword 'network'.

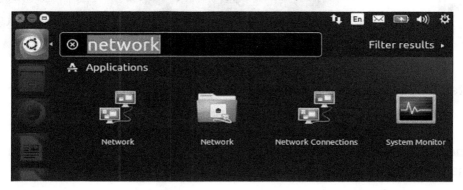

Step 2 − Double-click the Network icon. We can see the hostname assigned to the machine.

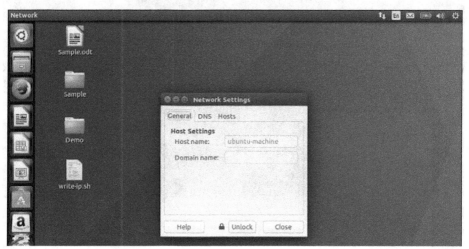

Step 3 – Click the Network folder option and we can see the IP address assigned to the machine.

Step 4 – Click the Options button and we can modify the details of the network connection.

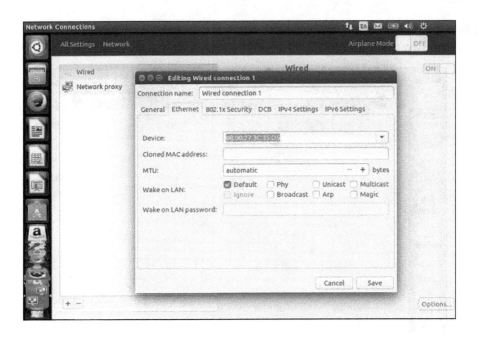

Ubuntu - Server Installation

Ubuntu also comes in a server version. This version is used for hosting applications such as webbased applications. The server version can be downloaded from the Ubuntu site in the same way as the desktop version of Ubuntu.

For the purpose of this tutorial, let's look at the installation of the server version 14.04, which is one of the most popular versions of Ubuntu. Following are the steps for installation.

Step 1 — Download for the server version from the link — http://releases.ubuntu.com/14.04/

Step 2 – Once the download of the server version is complete, put it on a USB device or bootable DVD. Boot the hardware from the bootable device.

Step 3 – The system prompts to select a language for the Installation. Select English and press the Enter button.

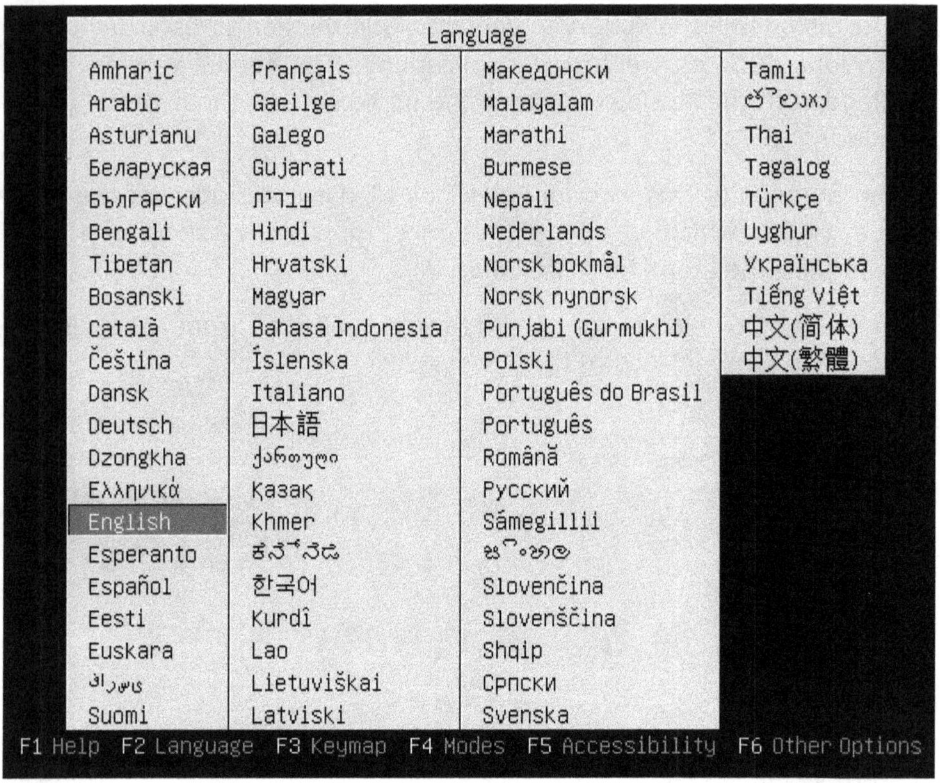

Language
Amharic
Arabic
Asturianu
Беларуская
Български
Bengali
Tibetan
Bosanski
Català
Čeština
Dansk
Deutsch
Dzongkha
Ελληνικά
English
Esperanto
Español
Eesti
Euskara
فارسی
Suomi
Français
Gaeilge
Galego
Gujarati
עברית
Hindi
Hrvatski
Magyar
Bahasa Indonesia
Íslenska
Italiano
日本語
ქართული
Қазақ
Khmer
ಕನ್ನಡ
한국어
Kurdî
Lao
Lietuviškai
Latviski
Македонски
Malayalam
Marathi
Burmese
Nepali
Nederlands
Norsk bokmål
Norsk nynorsk
Punjabi (Gurmukhi)
Polski
Português do Brasil
Português
Română
Русский
Sámegillii
සිංහල
Slovenčina
Slovenščina
Shqip
Српски
Svenska
Tamil
తెలుగు
Thai
Tagalog
Türkçe
Uyghur
Українська
Tiếng Việt
中文(简体)
中文(繁體)
F1 Help F2 Language F3 Keymap F4 Modes F5 Accessibility F6 Other Options

Step 4 − In the next step, choose the option to install Ubuntu server and press the Enter button.

ubuntu®

Install Ubuntu Server
Multiple server install with MAAS
Check disc for defects
Test memory
Boot from first hard disk
Rescue a broken system

F1 Help F2 Language F3 Keymap F4 Modes F5 Accessibility F6 Other Options

Step 5 — The system again prompts to select a language for the installation. Choose the English language and press the Enter button.

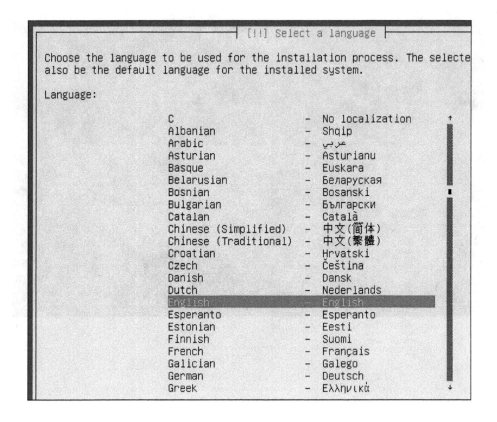

Step 6 – In the next screen, select the desired region and then press the Enter button.

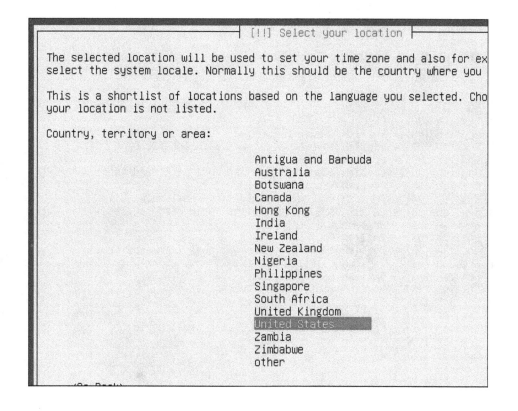

Step 7 – The next step includes the detection of the Keyboard layout. Choose the 'No' option and press the Enter button.

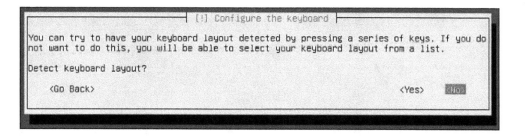

Step 8 – In the next screen, click the English(US) as the keyboard layout and press the Enter button.

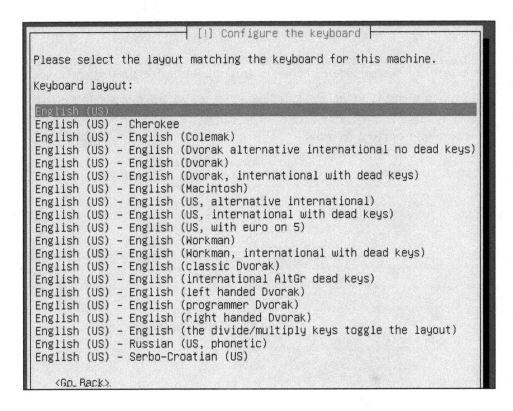

Step 9 – After performing a set of initial configuration steps, we will be prompted to enter a name for the system. Enter Ubuntuserver and press the Enter key.

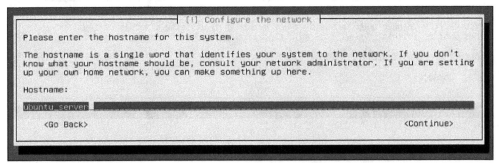

Step 10 – You will then be prompted to enter a real name and the username for an account to be created. Enter the name 'demo' and press Enter on both screens.

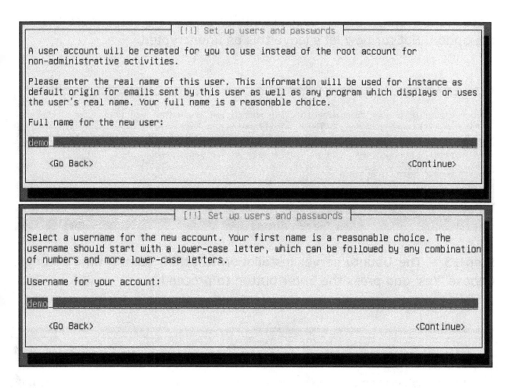

Step 11 – Now we need to enter a password for the new account. Enter a password and press the Enter button. The system will ask to verify the password.

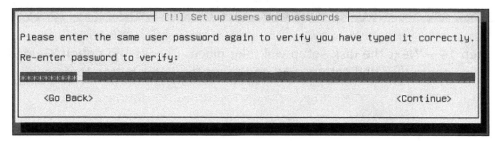

Step 12 – The system then asks if we want to encrypt the home directory. For the moment, let us say 'No' and press Enter to proceed. The encryption is such that if anyone does hack into the system, they will not be able steal the data as it is encrypted.

Once we are an advanced user of Ubuntu server, we can choose 'Yes' as the option. But for now let's leave this as unencrypted.

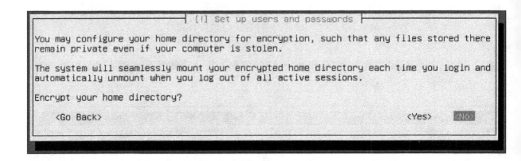

Step 13 – The Ubuntu server installation will then set the time settings. Choose 'Yes' and press the Enter button to proceed.

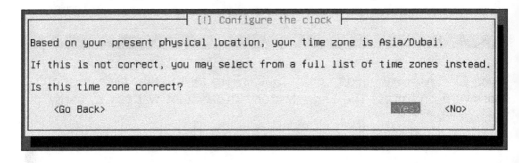

Step 14 – Next the disk setup will take place. Choose the option 'Guided – use entire disk and set up LVM' and press the Enter button to proceed.

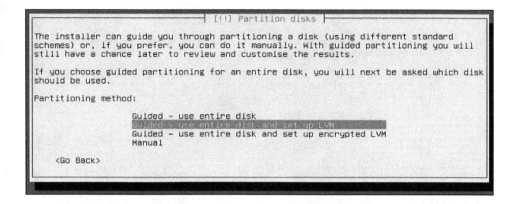

Step 15 – The installation will erase all the data on the disk. Since this is a fresh installation, this is not an issue. Click the Enter button to proceed.

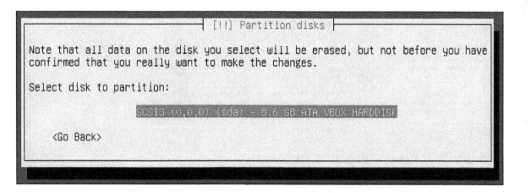

Step 16 – We will be asked to confirm all the changes to the disk. Choose the 'Yes' option and Press the Enter button to proceed.

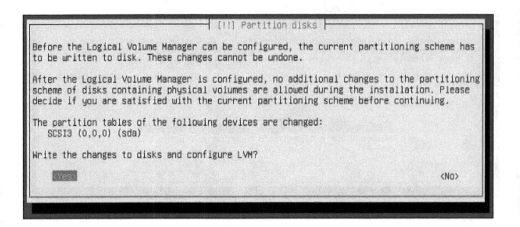

```
                        ┤ [!!] Partition disks ├
 Before the Logical Volume Manager can be configured, the current partitioning scheme has
 to be written to disk. These changes cannot be undone.

 After the Logical Volume Manager is configured, no additional changes to the partitioning
 scheme of disks containing physical volumes are allowed during the installation. Please
 decide if you are satisfied with the current partitioning scheme before continuing.

 The partition tables of the following devices are changed:
    SCSI3 (0,0,0) (sda)

 Write the changes to disks and configure LVM?

    <Yes>                                                                  <No>
```

Step 17 – The installation will detect the size of the hard disk. Hit the Enter button to proceed.

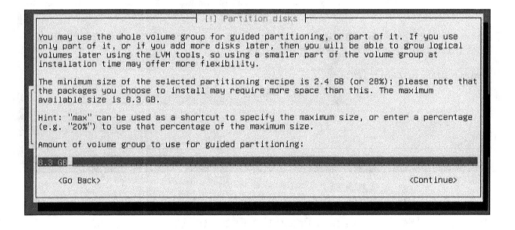

```
                        ┤ [!] Partition disks ├
 You may use the whole volume group for guided partitioning, or part of it. If you use
 only part of it, or if you add more disks later, then you will be able to grow logical
 volumes later using the LVM tools, so using a smaller part of the volume group at
 installation time may offer more flexibility.

 The minimum size of the selected partitioning recipe is 2.4 GB (or 28%); please note that
 the packages you choose to install may require more space than this. The maximum
 available size is 8.3 GB.

 Hint: "max" can be used as a shortcut to specify the maximum size, or enter a percentage
 (e.g. "20%") to use that percentage of the maximum size.

 Amount of volume group to use for guided partitioning:

 8.3 GB

    <Go Back>                                                        <Continue>
```

Step 18 – The system then asks to finalize the changes to the disk. Choose the 'Yes' option and press the 'Enter' button to proceed.

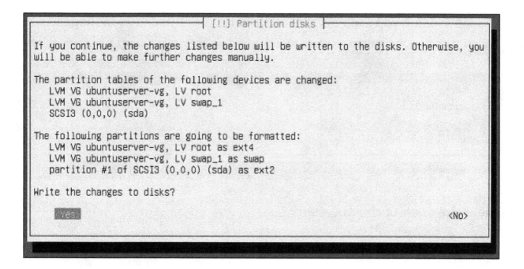

The system will then start performing a series of steps for the installation.

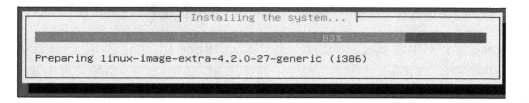

Step 19 − It will then ask to configure the Proxy setting. We can leave this setting as is and press the Enter button.

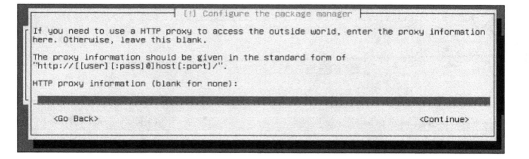

The installation will then start configuring the apt package manager.

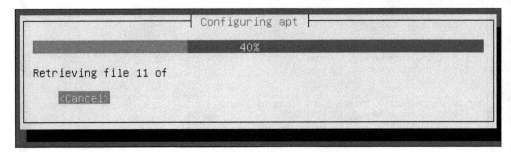

The installation of the necessary software will then start.

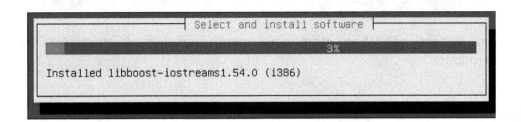

Step 20 – The system then asks if we want to configure automatic updates. For now, select 'No automatic updates' and press the Enter button.

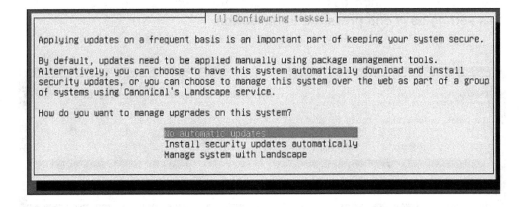

Step 21 – The next step is to install any additional software. Select 'OpenSSH' server which allows one to remotely connect to the server. Press the Enter button to proceed.

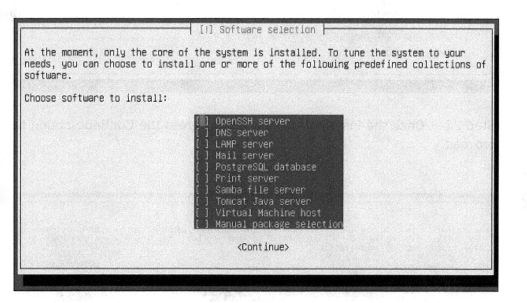

The system will start installing the remaining software on the system.

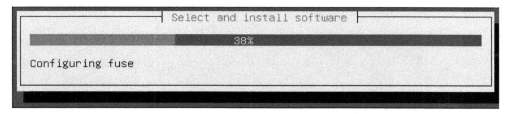

Step 22 – The system now requests to install the GRUB boot loader. Choose the 'Yes' option and press the Enter button to proceed.

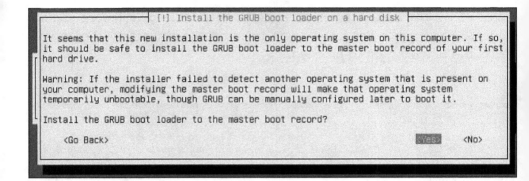

Step 23 — Once the installation is complete, press the Continue option to proceed.

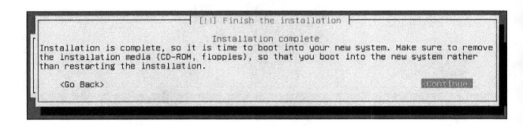

The system will then reboot after the installation.

```
[ 2034.931504] sd 2:0:0:0: [sda] Write Protect is off
[ 2034.932134] sd 2:0:0:0: [sda] Write cache: enabled, read cache: enabled, does
n't support DPO or FUA
[ 2034.934712]  sda: sda1 sda2 < sda5 >
[ 2034.935538] sd 2:0:0:0: [sda] Attached SCSI disk
[ 2035.008210] tsc: Refined TSC clocksource calibration: 2494.392 MHz
[ 2035.009669] clocksource: tsc: mask: 0xffffffffffffffff max_cycles: 0x23f48811
765, max_idle_ns: 440795220701 ns
[ 2035.127599] usb 1-1: New USB device found, idVendor=80ee, idProduct=0021
[ 2035.129104] usb 1-1: New USB device strings: Mfr=1, Product=3, SerialNumber=0
[ 2035.129795] usb 1-1: Product: USB Tablet
[ 2035.130486] usb 1-1: Manufacturer: VirtualBox
[ 2035.140161] hidraw: raw HID events driver (C) Jiri Kosina
[ 2035.155988] usbcore: registered new interface driver usbhid
[ 2035.157392] usbhid: USB HID core driver
[ 2035.164713] input: VirtualBox USB Tablet as /devices/pci0000:00/0000:00:06.0/
usb1/1-1/1-1:1.0/0003:80EE:0021.0001/input/input5
[ 2035.166702] hid-generic 0003:80EE:0021.0001: input,hidraw0: USB HID v1.10 Mou
se [VirtualBox USB Tablet] on usb-0000:00:06.0-1/input0
[ 2035.337911] random: lvm urandom read with 21 bits of entropy available
Begin: Running /scripts/local-premount ... done.
[ 2036.258973] EXT4-fs (dm-0): mounted filesystem with ordered data mode. Opts:
(null)
Begin: Running /scripts/local-bottom ... done.
done.
Begin: Running /scripts/init-bottom ... [ 2037.496563] floppy0: no floppy contro
llers found
done.
[ 2039.740585] random: nonblocking pool is initialized
```

Step 24 — We will then be requested to log into the system. Enter the credentials which were entered at the time of installation.

```
Ubuntu 14.04.4 LTS ubuntuserver tty1

ubuntuserver login: demo
Password:
```

We will finally be logged into the system.

```
Ubuntu 14.04.4 LTS ubuntuserver tty1

ubuntuserver login: demo
Password:
Welcome to Ubuntu 14.04.4 LTS (GNU/Linux 4.2.0-27-generic i686)

 * Documentation:  https://help.ubuntu.com/

  System information as of Sat Sep 24 02:25:53 GST 2016

  System load:  1.08               Processes:            93
  Usage of /:   15.8% of 6.12GB     Users logged in:      0
  Memory usage: 3%                  IP address for eth0: 10.0.2.15
  Swap usage:   0%

  Graph this data and manage this system at:
    https://landscape.canonical.com/

90 packages can be updated.
55 updates are security updates.


The programs included with the Ubuntu system are free software;
the exact distribution terms for each program are described in the
individual files in /usr/share/doc/*/copyright.

Ubuntu comes with ABSOLUTELY NO WARRANTY, to the extent permitted by
applicable law.

demo@ubuntuserver:~$
```

We have successfully installed the server version of Ubuntu.

UBUNTU - SECURE SHELL

The Secure Shell (SSH) in Linux is used to log into the machine in an encrypted and safe manner. This helps in providing a secure channel to streamline all requests to the Ubuntu server. SSH uses cryptographic keys to log into the server.

On Windows, the most common tool to perform a secure shell to a Linux server is putty. In this chapter, we will learn how to use putty to Secure Shell into a server.

Step 1 − Download putty from the http://www.putty.org/ site.

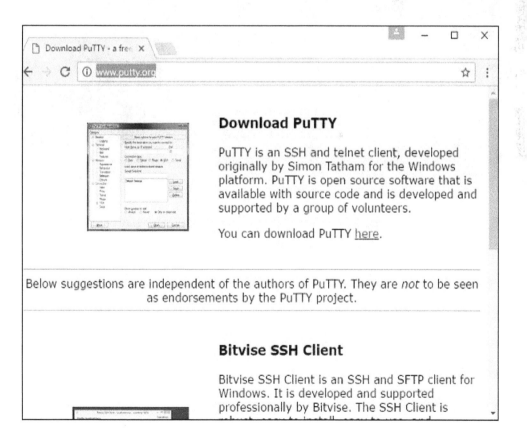

Step 2 − Before connecting to use putty, we need to know the IP address of our Ubuntu box. To do this, type ifconfig in the command shell of the Ubuntu server.

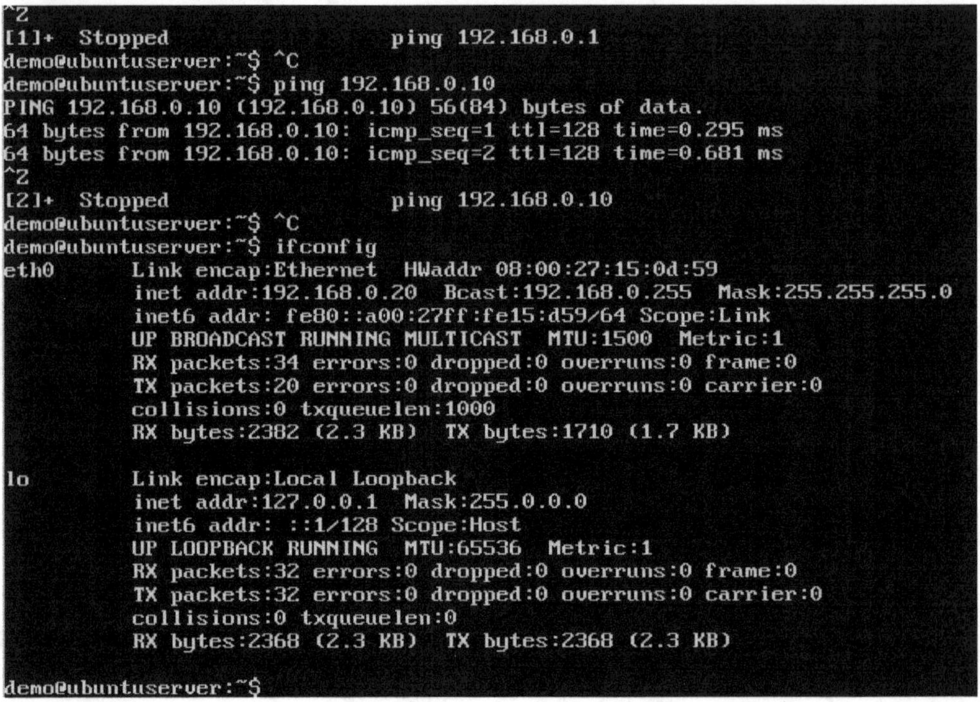

```
^Z
[1]+  Stopped                      ping 192.168.0.1
demo@ubuntuserver:~$ ^C
demo@ubuntuserver:~$ ping 192.168.0.10
PING 192.168.0.10 (192.168.0.10) 56(84) bytes of data.
64 bytes from 192.168.0.10: icmp_seq=1 ttl=128 time=0.295 ms
64 bytes from 192.168.0.10: icmp_seq=2 ttl=128 time=0.681 ms
^Z
[2]+  Stopped                      ping 192.168.0.10
demo@ubuntuserver:~$ ^C
demo@ubuntuserver:~$ ifconfig
eth0      Link encap:Ethernet  HWaddr 08:00:27:15:0d:59
          inet addr:192.168.0.20  Bcast:192.168.0.255  Mask:255.255.255.0
          inet6 addr: fe80::a00:27ff:fe15:d59/64 Scope:Link
          UP BROADCAST RUNNING MULTICAST  MTU:1500  Metric:1
          RX packets:34 errors:0 dropped:0 overruns:0 frame:0
          TX packets:20 errors:0 dropped:0 overruns:0 carrier:0
          collisions:0 txqueuelen:1000
          RX bytes:2382 (2.3 KB)  TX bytes:1710 (1.7 KB)

lo        Link encap:Local Loopback
          inet addr:127.0.0.1  Mask:255.0.0.0
          inet6 addr: ::1/128 Scope:Host
          UP LOOPBACK RUNNING  MTU:65536  Metric:1
          RX packets:32 errors:0 dropped:0 overruns:0 frame:0
          TX packets:32 errors:0 dropped:0 overruns:0 carrier:0
          collisions:0 txqueuelen:0
          RX bytes:2368 (2.3 KB)  TX bytes:2368 (2.3 KB)

demo@ubuntuserver:~$
```

From the above screenshot, we know that the IP address of the server is 192.168.0.20

142

Step 3 — Next step is installing SSH on the server. In order to SSH to a server, you need to make sure it is installed. Run the following command in the Ubuntu server command prompt session.

sudo apt-get install openssh-server

```
Ubuntu 14.04.4 LTS ubuntuserver tty1

ubuntuserver login: demo
Password:
Last login: Tue Oct 11 10:43:23 GST 2016 on tty1
Welcome to Ubuntu 14.04.4 LTS (GNU/Linux 4.2.0-27-generic i686)

 * Documentation:  https://help.ubuntu.com/

   System information as of Tue Oct 11 11:09:45 GST 2016

   System load: 0.08              Memory usage: 2%   Processes:          75
   Usage of /:  17.8% of 6.12GB   Swap usage:   0%   Users logged in: 0

   Graph this data and manage this system at:
     https://landscape.canonical.com/

New release '16.04.1 LTS' available.
Run 'do-release-upgrade' to upgrade to it.

demo@ubuntuserver:~$ sudo apt-get install openssh-server
```

Step 4 — Launch PuTTY. Enter the IP address of the Ubuntu server and click the Open button.

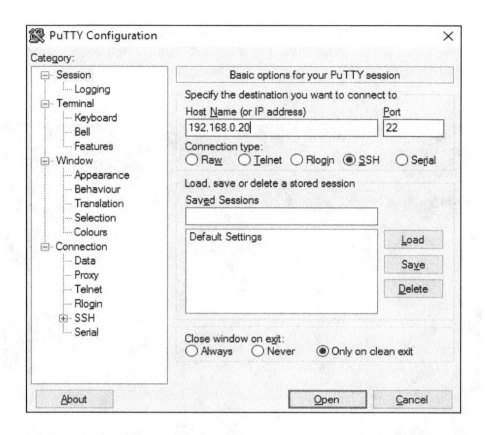

Step 5 – The next screen requests to accept the encrypted key sent from the server.

144

Step 6 – Finally, enter the username and password to log into the server. We have successfully established a secure shell to the server.

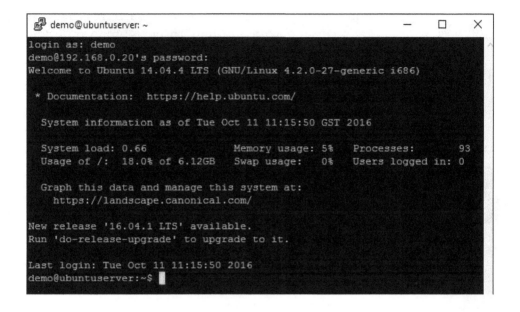

UBUNTU - DEVELOPMENT

The Ubuntu desktop edition can be used to develop web applications. One of the most famous software which can be used for development on Ubuntu is Aptana. Let's see the steps on how to get Aptana and get a simple web project up and running.

Step 1 – On Ubuntu desktop, open Firefox and go to the url – http://www.aptana.com/products/studio3/download

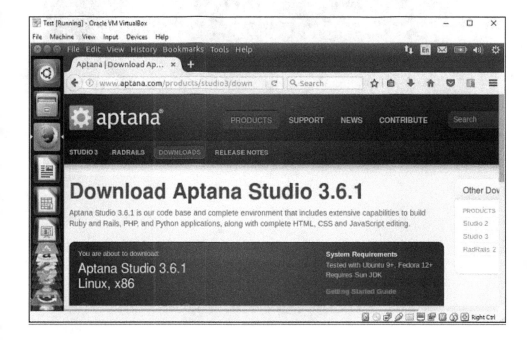

Step 2 − Click the Download Aptana Studio 3 button.

Step 3 − Once downloaded, extract the zip file to a suitable location. Once extracted, click the AptanaStudio3 link.

The following interface pops up. We can then choose to create a new web project, if required.

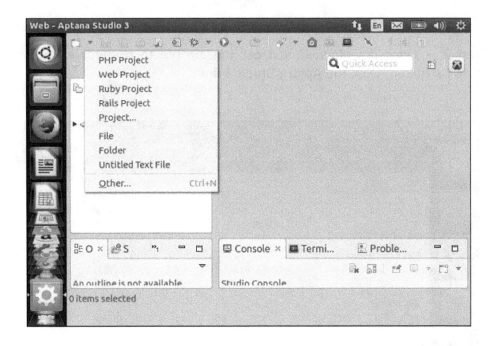

The required development can be carried out on the web project.

Ubuntu - Nginx

Nginx is a much lighter web server than Apache. This web server has become quite popular in the recent years. The Apache web server can be quite complex to configure and use. However, Nginx is much simpler. This chapter will focus on how to install this light web server.

To install Nginx, following are the steps —

Step 1 — Open the command terminal on Ubuntu desktop and run the following command.

sudo apt-get update

This first ensures that all packages on the operating system are up to date.

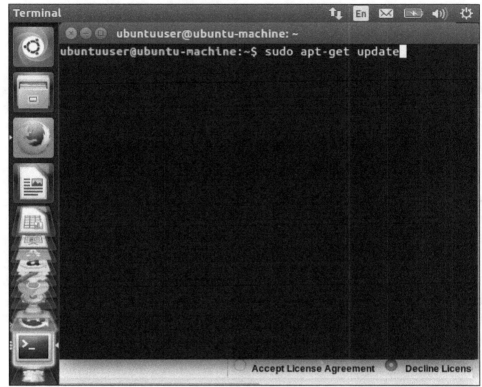

Step 2 – Next enter the following command to install the nginx server.

sudo apt-get install nginx

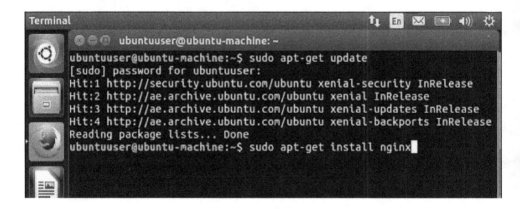

Step 3 – Once done, if we run ps –ef | grep nginx, we can see the process for the web server in a running state.

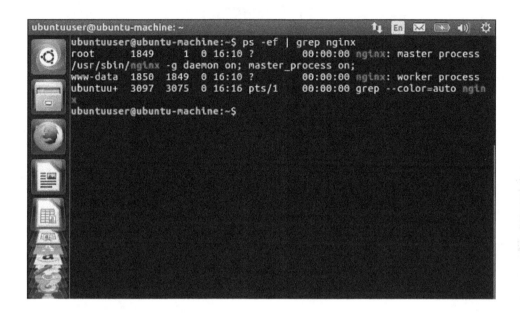

We now have nginx run as a web server on Ubuntu.

UBUNTU - VIRTUAL MACHINES

Ubuntu can also be installed as virtual machines. Some of the software which support virtual machines are –

- Microsoft Hyper-V
- VMWare Workstation
- Oracle VirtualBox

Let's use Oracle VirtualBox to create our Ubuntu virtual machine. Oracle VirtualBox is a free tool from Oracle. Following are the steps to have the virtual machine in place.

Step 1 – Download Oracle VirtualBox from the oracle site – https://www.virtualbox.org/

Step 2 — Go to the downloads section and download the Windows version.

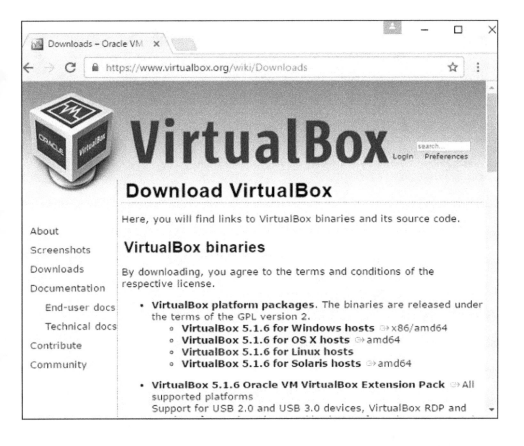

Step 3 — Once download is complete, install VirtualBox. Launch the installer. Click the Run button on the following screen.

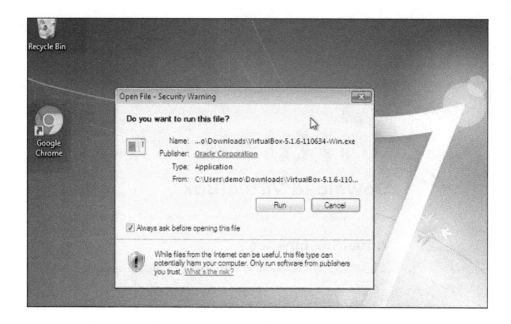

Step 4 — Click the Next button on the subsequent screen.

Step 5 – Choose the appropriate folder location and click the Next button.

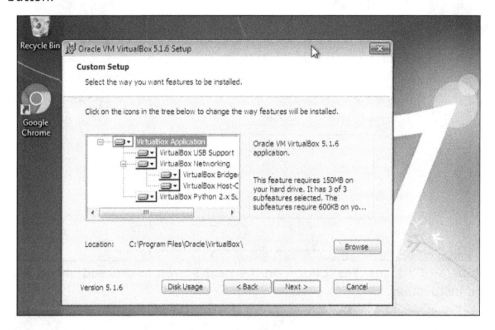

Step 6 – Click Next on the subsequent screen.

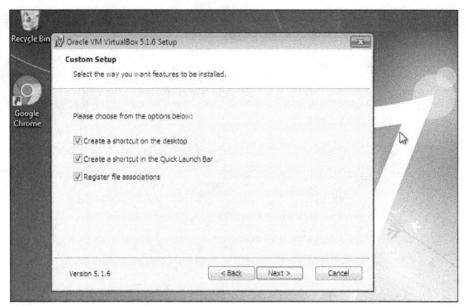

Step 7 — Click the 'Yes' button on the next screen to proceed ahead with the installation.

Step 8 — Click Install on the next screen.

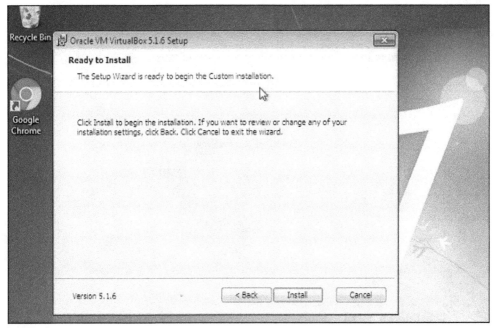

Step 9 − After the installation is complete, launch Oracle VirtualBox. On the Launch screen, click the 'New' menu option.

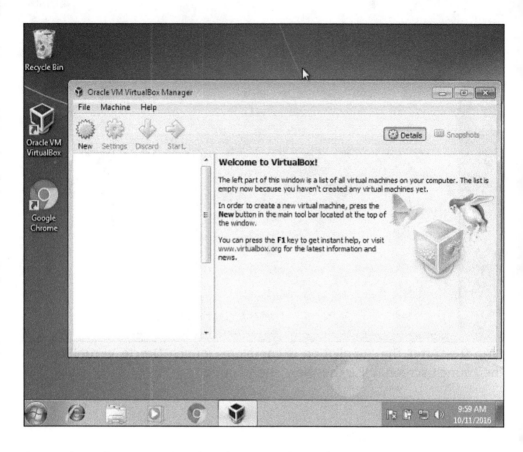

Step 10 — Give a name for the virtual machine and give the type as Ubuntu and then click the Next button.

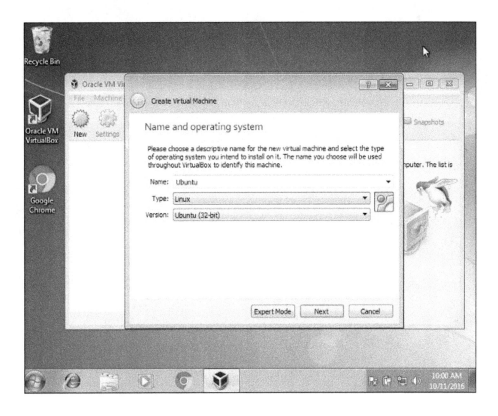

Step 11 − In the next screen, keep the recommended RAM as it is and click the Next button.

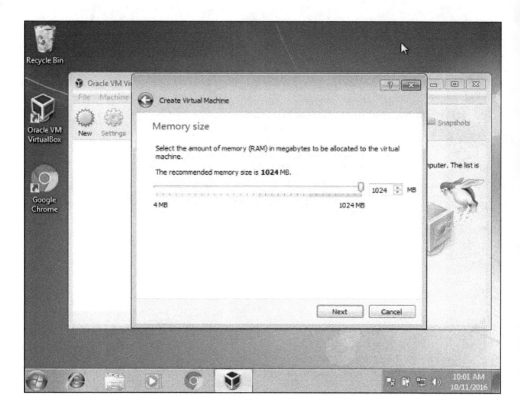

Step 12 — Accept the default setting for the virtual hard disk and click the Create button.

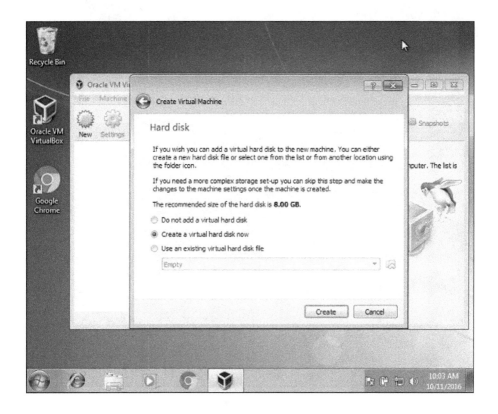

Step 13 – Accept the hard disk type and click the Next button.

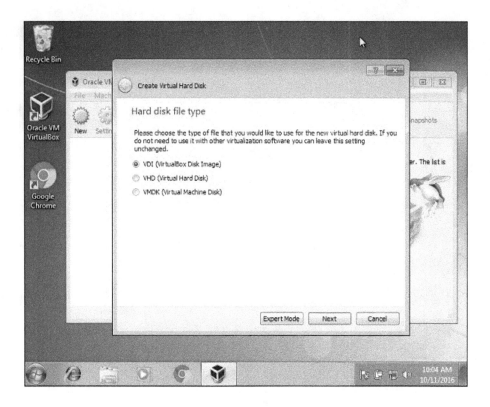

Step 14 – Accept the default type of physical hard disk allocation and click the Next button.

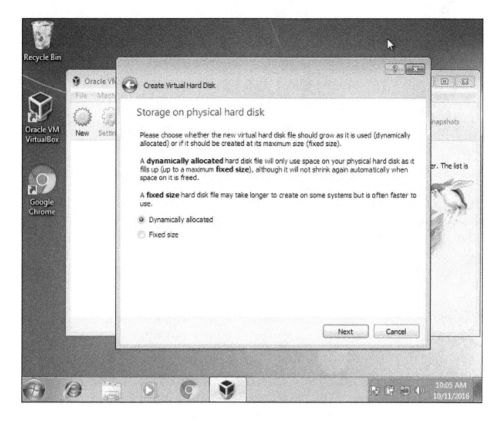

Step 15 — Accept the default file location and click the Create button.

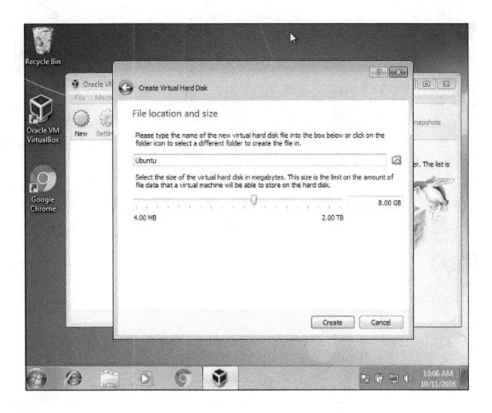

Step 16 — Now that the Virtual Machine has been created, click the Settings Menu option.

Step 17 – Go to the Storage option, click the Empty disk icon and browse for the Ubuntu iso image. Then click the OK button.

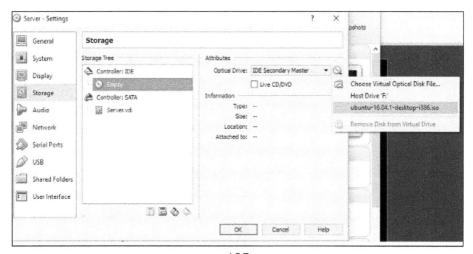

165

Finally click the Start button. The system prompts to install Ubuntu. Follow the steps in the Installation chapter and we will have a Virtual Machine hosting Ubuntu.

Ubuntu - Installing MySQL and Python

MySQL and Python are famous database and development software respectively. These are normally installed on Linux-based systems. Let's see how we can get them installed on Ubuntu server environments.

Installing Python

The first thing to do is to find out what is the version of Python installed on the system. We can find this issuing the following command.

```
Python –v
```

Where the –v option specifies to show what is the version of Python installed. The following screenshot shows a sample of the output of the above command.

```
a.py
import _sysconfigdata # precompiled from /usr/lib/python2.7/_sysconfigdata.pyc
# /usr/lib/python2.7/plat-i386-linux-gnu/_sysconfigdata_nd.pyc matches /usr/lib/
python2.7/plat-i386-linux-gnu/_sysconfigdata_nd.py
import _sysconfigdata_nd # precompiled from /usr/lib/python2.7/plat-i386-linux-g
nu/_sysconfigdata_nd.pyc
# /usr/lib/python2.7/sitecustomize.pyc matches /usr/lib/python2.7/sitecustomize.
py
import sitecustomize # precompiled from /usr/lib/python2.7/sitecustomize.pyc
import encodings # directory /usr/lib/python2.7/encodings
# /usr/lib/python2.7/encodings/__init__.pyc matches /usr/lib/python2.7/encodings
/__init__.py
import encodings # precompiled from /usr/lib/python2.7/encodings/__init__.pyc
# /usr/lib/python2.7/codecs.pyc matches /usr/lib/python2.7/codecs.py
import codecs # precompiled from /usr/lib/python2.7/codecs.pyc
import _codecs # builtin
# /usr/lib/python2.7/encodings/aliases.pyc matches /usr/lib/python2.7/encodings/
aliases.py
import encodings.aliases # precompiled from /usr/lib/python2.7/encodings/aliases
.pyc
# /usr/lib/python2.7/encodings/utf_8.pyc matches /usr/lib/python2.7/encodings/ut
f_8.py
import encodings.utf_8 # precompiled from /usr/lib/python2.7/encodings/utf_8.pyc
Python 2.7.6 (default, Jun 22 2015, 18:00:18)
[GCC 4.8.2] on linux2
Type "help", "copyright", "credits" or "license" for more information.
dlopen("/usr/lib/python2.7/lib-dynload/readline.i386-linux-gnu.so", 2);
import readline # dynamically loaded from /usr/lib/python2.7/lib-dynload/readlin
e.i386-linux-gnu.so
>>>
```

From the above output, we can see that the version of Python installed is version 2.7.

There is another way to see if Python is installed via the following commands.

Python –V

Python3 –V

The later command is used to see the version 3 of Python installed.

```
demo@ubuntuserver:~$ python3 -V
Python 3.4.3
demo@ubuntuserver:~$ python -V
Python 2.7.6
demo@ubuntuserver:~$
```

If we want to have the latest version of Python installed, then we need to issue the following statement.

sudo apt-get install python3

The above command will download the necessary packages for Python and have it installed.

INSTALLING MYSQL

To install MySQL, the following steps need to be followed.

Step 1 – Issue the apt-get command to ensure all operating system packages are up to date.

sudo apt-get update

```
1,215 B]
Get:38 http://us.archive.ubuntu.com trusty-backports/restricted Translation-en
28 B]
Get:39 http://us.archive.ubuntu.com trusty-backports/universe Translation-en [
.8 kB]
Hit http://us.archive.ubuntu.com trusty Release
Hit http://us.archive.ubuntu.com trusty/main Sources
Hit http://us.archive.ubuntu.com trusty/restricted Sources
Hit http://us.archive.ubuntu.com trusty/universe Sources
Hit http://us.archive.ubuntu.com trusty/multiverse Sources
Hit http://us.archive.ubuntu.com trusty/main i386 Packages
Hit http://us.archive.ubuntu.com trusty/restricted i386 Packages
Hit http://us.archive.ubuntu.com trusty/universe i386 Packages
Hit http://us.archive.ubuntu.com trusty/multiverse i386 Packages
Hit http://us.archive.ubuntu.com trusty/main Translation-en
Hit http://us.archive.ubuntu.com trusty/multiverse Translation-en
Hit http://us.archive.ubuntu.com trusty/restricted Translation-en
Hit http://us.archive.ubuntu.com trusty/universe Translation-en
Ign http://us.archive.ubuntu.com trusty/main Translation-en_US
Ign http://us.archive.ubuntu.com trusty/multiverse Translation-en_US
Ign http://us.archive.ubuntu.com trusty/restricted Translation-en_US
Ign http://us.archive.ubuntu.com trusty/universe Translation-en_US
Fetched 4,027 kB in 30s (134 kB/s)
Reading package lists... Done
demo@ubuntuserver:~$
```

Step 2 – Once all the packages have been updated, it is time to get the packages for MySQL.

sudo apt-get install mysql-server

The above command will start the download of all the relevant packages for MySQL.

Once the download completes and the installation starts, the installer will first ask to configure a root password.

Step 3 – Enter the required password and click the OK button. It will also prompt to re-enter the password.

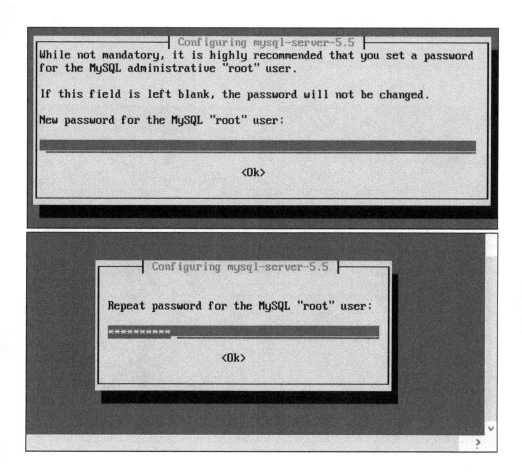

Step 4 – To see the MySQL process running, run the following command.

```
ps –ef | grep mysql
```

The following screenshot shows mysqld which is the daemon process for mysql running in the background.

```
demo@ubuntuserver:~$ ps -ef | grep mysql
mysql      2715      1  0 15:06 ?        00:00:00 /usr/sbin/mysqld
demo       2885   1035  0 15:07 tty1     00:00:00 grep --color=auto mysql
demo@ubuntuserver:~$ _
```

Step 5 – To configure mysql, run the following command.

/usr/bin/mysql_secure_installation

```
demo@ubuntuserver:~$ ps -ef | grep mysql
mysql      2715      1  0 15:06 ?        00:00:00 /usr/sbin/mysqld
demo       2885   1035  0 15:07 tty1     00:00:00 grep --color=auto mysql
demo@ubuntuserver:~$ /usr/bin/mysql_secure_installation




NOTE: RUNNING ALL PARTS OF THIS SCRIPT IS RECOMMENDED FOR ALL MySQL
      SERVERS IN PRODUCTION USE!  PLEASE READ EACH STEP CAREFULLY!


In order to log into MySQL to secure it, we'll need the current
password for the root user.  If you've just installed MySQL, and
you haven't set the root password yet, the password will be blank,
so you should just press enter here.

Enter current password for root (enter for none):
```

It prompts to enter the root password which was entered during the installation process.

Step 6 – Enter the password and hit Enter.

Now, it prompts on whether we want to change the root password.

Step 7 – Enter 'N' for No and proceed.

Again, it prompts on whether we want to remove the Anonymous access.

```
You already have a root password set, so you can safely answer 'n'.

Change the root password? [Y/n] n
 ... skipping.

By default, a MySQL installation has an anonymous user, allowing anyone
to log into MySQL without having to have a user account created for
them. This is intended only for testing, and to make the installation
go a bit smoother. You should remove them before moving into a
production environment.

Remove anonymous users? [Y/n] n
 ... skipping.

Normally, root should only be allowed to connect from 'localhost'. This
ensures that someone cannot guess at the root password from the network.

Disallow root login remotely? [Y/n] n
 ... skipping.

By default, MySQL comes with a database named 'test' that anyone can
access. This is also intended only for testing, and should be removed
before moving into a production environment.

Remove test database and access to it? [Y/n]
```

Step 8 – When connecting from other machines on this database, it is advised to keep the default options as 'N' for both anonymous users and disallow root login remotely.

```
By default, MySQL comes with a database named 'test' that anyone can
access.  This is also intended only for testing, and should be removed
before moving into a production environment.

Remove test database and access to it? [Y/n] n
 ... skipping.

Reloading the privilege tables will ensure that all changes made so far
will take effect immediately.

Reload privilege tables now? [Y/n] Y
 ... Success!

Cleaning up...


All done!  If you've completed all of the above steps, your MySQL
installation should now be secure.

Thanks for using MySQL!

demo@ubuntuserver:~$
```

Step 9 – It is advised to provide the option as No for the options of
Remove test database as well. We can enter 'Y' to reload the privileges
table.

Finally, the configuration of MySQL will be complete.

Ubuntu - Node.js

Node.js is a popular JavaScript framework used for developing server side applications. In this chapter, we will see how to get Node.js installed on Ubuntu.

Following are the steps to get Node.js installed.

Step 1 – Run the following command.

sudo apt-get install nodejs

This will install all the necessary packages for Node.js

```
Unpacking node-jsv (4.0.0+ds1-1) ...
Processing triggers for man-db (2.6.7.1-1ubuntu1) ...
Setting up libc-ares2:i386 (1.10.0-2) ...
Setting up javascript-common (11) ...
Setting up libjs-node-uuid (1.4.0-1) ...
Setting up libv8-3.14.5 (3.14.5.8-5ubuntu2) ...
Setting up nodejs (0.10.25~dfsg2-2ubuntu1) ...
update-alternatives: using /usr/bin/nodejs to provide /usr/bin/js (js) in auto m
ode
Setting up node-async (0.2.5-1) ...
Setting up node-cli (0.4.4~20120516-1) ...
Setting up node-jsconfig (0.2.0-1) ...
Setting up node-node-uuid (1.4.0-1) ...
Setting up node-delayed-stream (0.0.5-1) ...
Setting up node-combined-stream (0.0.4-1) ...
Setting up node-contextify (0.1.6-1) ...
Setting up node-cookie-jar (0.3.1-1) ...
Setting up node-cssom (0.3.0-1) ...
Setting up node-forever-agent (0.5.1-1) ...
Setting up node-mime (1.2.11-1) ...
Setting up node-form-data (0.1.0-1) ...
Setting up node-htmlparser (1.7.5+ds1-1) ...
Setting up node-tunnel-agent (0.3.1-1) ...
Setting up node-json-stringify-safe (5.0.0-1) ...
Setting up node-qs (0.6.5-1) ...
Setting up node-request (2.26.1-1) ...
Setting up node-jsdom (0.8.10+dfsg1-1) ...
Setting up node-jsv (4.0.0+ds1-1) ...
Processing triggers for libc-bin (2.19-0ubuntu6.7) ...
demo@ubuntuserver:~$
```

Next, we need to install the Node package manager which is required for Node.js applications.

175

Step 2 – Run the following command.

```
sudo apt-get install npm
```

All the necessary packages for the node package manager will be installed.

```
Setting up node-mkdirp (0.3.5-1) ...
Setting up node-graceful-fs (2.0.0-2) ...
Setting up node-fstream (0.1.24-1) ...
Setting up node-lru-cache (2.3.1-1) ...
Setting up node-sigmund (1.0.0-1) ...
Setting up node-minimatch (0.2.12-1) ...
Setting up node-fstream-ignore (0.0.6-2) ...
Setting up node-github-url-from-git (1.1.1-1) ...
Setting up node-glob (3.2.6-1) ...
Setting up nodejs-dev (0.10.25~dfsg2-2ubuntu1) ...
Setting up node-nopt (2.1.2-1) ...
Setting up node-npmlog (0.0.4-1) ...
Setting up node-osenv (0.0.3-1) ...
Setting up node-semver (2.1.0-2) ...
Setting up node-tar (0.1.18-1) ...
Setting up node-which (1.0.5-2) ...
Setting up node-gyp (0.10.10-2) ...
Setting up node-ini (1.1.0-1) ...
Setting up node-lockfile (0.4.1-1) ...
Setting up node-mute-stream (0.0.3-1) ...
Setting up node-normalize-package-data (0.2.2-1) ...
Setting up node-once (1.1.1-1) ...
Setting up node-read (1.0.4-1) ...
Setting up node-read-package-json (1.1.3-1) ...
Setting up node-retry (0.6.0-1) ...
Setting up node-sha (1.2.3-1) ...
Setting up node-slide (1.1.4-1) ...
Setting up npm (1.3.10~dfsg-1) ...
Processing triggers for libc-bin (2.19-0ubuntu6.7) ...
demo@ubuntuserver:~$
```

Step 3 – Next, create a symbolic link to the Node.js folder. Then, run the Node –v command and npm –v to see the Node and npm version installed.

```
demo@ubuntuserver:~$ sudo ln -s /usr/bin/nodejs /usr/bin/node
demo@ubuntuserver:~$ node -v
v0.10.25
demo@ubuntuserver:~$ npm-v
npm-v: command not found
demo@ubuntuserver:~$ npm -v
1.3.10
demo@ubuntuserver:~$ _
```

UBUNTU - DOCKER

Docker is a container service which allows one to run applications or even operating systems on a host operating system as containers. Containers are a new and exciting technology that has evolved over the last couple of years and being adopted by a lot of key organizations.

Docker is a company that develops these special containers for applications. The official website for Docker is https://www.docker.com/

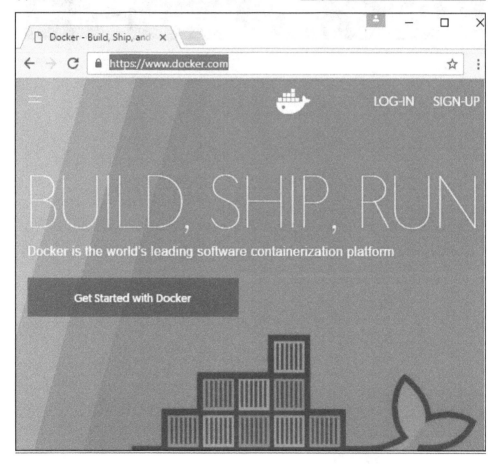

As an exercise, let's install a CentOS container on an Ubuntu system. CentOS is a Linux-based operating system from Red Hat. Thus, we will be running the CentOS system on top of Ubuntu. Following are the steps to have this in place.

Step 1 – The first step is to install the Docker application on Ubuntu server. Thus on the Ubuntu test server, run the following command to ensure that OS updates are in place.

sudo apt-get update

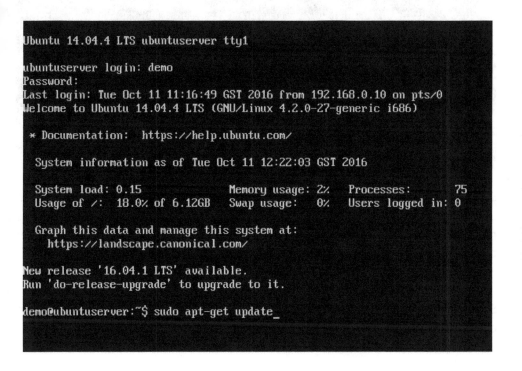

Step 2 – Once all updates have been processed, issue the following command to get Docker installed.

sudo apt-get install -y docker.io

```
Hit http://us.archive.ubuntu.com trusty-backports/universe Sources
Hit http://us.archive.ubuntu.com trusty-backports/multiverse Sources
Hit http://us.archive.ubuntu.com trusty-backports/main i386 Packages
Hit http://us.archive.ubuntu.com trusty-backports/restricted i386 Packages
Hit http://us.archive.ubuntu.com trusty-backports/universe i386 Packages
Hit http://us.archive.ubuntu.com trusty-backports/multiverse i386 Packages
Hit http://us.archive.ubuntu.com trusty-backports/main Translation-en
Hit http://us.archive.ubuntu.com trusty-backports/multiverse Translation-en
Hit http://us.archive.ubuntu.com trusty-backports/restricted Translation-en
Hit http://us.archive.ubuntu.com trusty-backports/universe Translation-en
Hit http://us.archive.ubuntu.com trusty Release
Hit http://us.archive.ubuntu.com trusty/main Sources
Hit http://us.archive.ubuntu.com trusty/restricted Sources
Hit http://us.archive.ubuntu.com trusty/universe Sources
Hit http://us.archive.ubuntu.com trusty/multiverse Sources
Hit http://us.archive.ubuntu.com trusty/main i386 Packages
Hit http://us.archive.ubuntu.com trusty/restricted i386 Packages
Hit http://us.archive.ubuntu.com trusty/universe i386 Packages
Hit http://us.archive.ubuntu.com trusty/multiverse i386 Packages
Hit http://us.archive.ubuntu.com trusty/main Translation-en
Hit http://us.archive.ubuntu.com trusty/multiverse Translation-en
Hit http://us.archive.ubuntu.com trusty/restricted Translation-en
Hit http://us.archive.ubuntu.com trusty/universe Translation-en
Ign http://us.archive.ubuntu.com trusty/main Translation-en_US
Ign http://us.archive.ubuntu.com trusty/multiverse Translation-en_US
Ign http://us.archive.ubuntu.com trusty/restricted Translation-en_US
Ign http://us.archive.ubuntu.com trusty/universe Translation-en_US
Fetched 3,826 kB in 1min 6s (57.3 kB/s)
Reading package lists... Done
demo@ubuntuserver:~$ sudo apt-get install -y docker.io
```

Step 3 – Once the Docker packages are installed, we should receive an output message stating that the Docker process has started and is running. The Docker process is known as the Docker engine or Docker daemon.

Step 4 – To view the version of Docker running, issue the Docker info command.

```
demo@ubuntuserver:~$ sudo docker info
Containers: 0
Images: 0
Storage Driver: aufs
 Root Dir: /var/lib/docker/aufs
 Backing Filesystem: extfs
 Dirs: 0
 Dirperm1 Supported: true
Execution Driver: native-0.2
Kernel Version: 4.2.0-27-generic
Operating System: Ubuntu 14.04.4 LTS
CPUs: 1
Total Memory: 1.354 GiB
Name: ubuntuserver
ID: M4VC:QDHQ:QYJF:LXH7:6EZM:3APY:YJ3Y:YF6C:JATV:2WVD:SQJL:SPKN
WARNING: No swap limit support
demo@ubuntuserver:~$ _
```

Step 5 − The next step is to install our CentOS image on Ubuntu.

Docker has a special site called the Docker hub, which is used to store pre-built images for Docker. The link to the site is https://hub.docker.com/

Step 6 − Do a quick and simple sign-in process to be able to log into the site and see all the available Docker images.

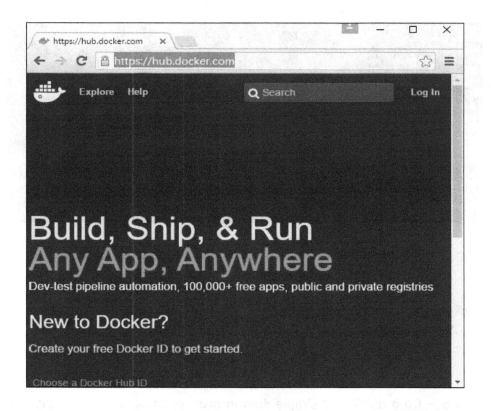

Step 7 – Once logged in, click the Explore button to see all the available Docker images.

The two important points to note are −

- The Docker pull command. This is the command to install the Docker image on Linux box.
- The Docker details for the various versions of CentOS.

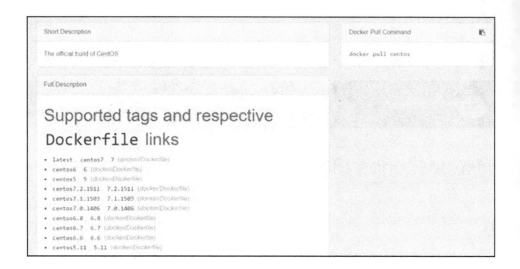

Step 8 − On Ubuntu box, run the command.

sudo docker pull centos:latest

The download of the Docker component starts and the CentOS Docker is downloaded. The name of the Docker image is centos:latest, which means that we have the latest Docker image for CentOS.

Step 9 − To see all the Docker images installed, issue the command

sudo docker images

In the following screenshot, we can see that the Docker image is just 196.8 MB in size, and this is the subset of the CentOS which now runs on Ubuntu system.

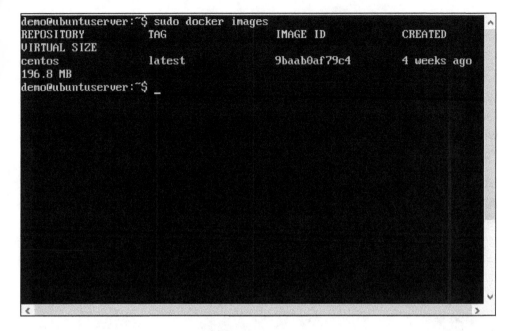

```
demo@ubuntuserver:~$ sudo docker images
REPOSITORY              TAG              IMAGE ID          CREATED
VIRTUAL SIZE
centos                  latest           9baab0af79c4      4 weeks ago
196.8 MB
demo@ubuntuserver:~$ _
```

Step 10 − To start CentOS, we need to issue a command to the OS to get a thread started. We can do this by running the following command.

sudo docker run -it centos /bin/bash

The above command does the following things −

- Runs the CentOS Docker image.
- Runs the image in interactive mode by using the -it option.
- Runs the /bin/bash command as the initial process.

Ubuntu - On the Cloud

We can also install Ubuntu on various cloud environments such as Google Cloud, Amazon web services, and Azure web services. In this chapter, we will see how to get Ubuntu up and running on Amazon web services. Following are the steps to get this in place.

Step 1 − One can get a free account with Amazon web services. All we need to do is register with AWS on the following url − https://aws.amazon.com/

Step 2 − Click the Sign in to the Console and it presents the following dialog box.

Step 3 — Click the option 'I am a new user' and enter the required email id of an existing Gmail account. Then click the 'Sign in using our secure server' button. We will then need to give some information in the subsequent screen to create an account.

Step 4 — Once an account has been created, we can log into the console. Once logged in, click the EC2 option. This option is used for creating virtual machines on the cloud.

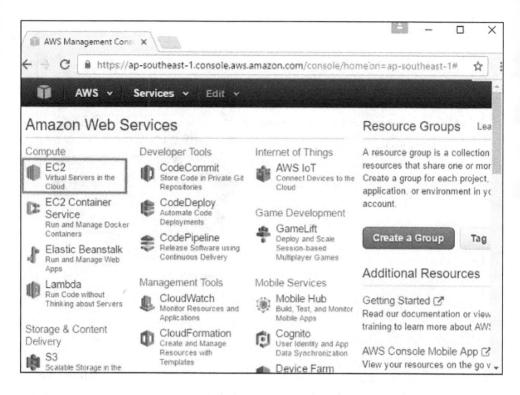

Step 5 — In the following screenshot, click the Launch Instance button.

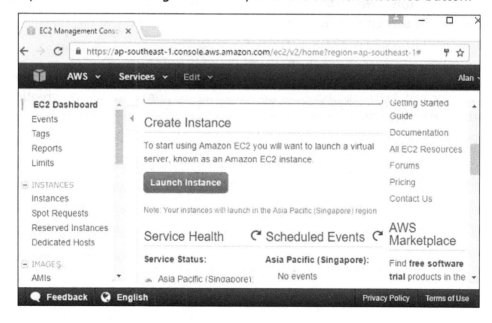

Step 6 – The next screen prompts to select an appropriate AMI. An AMI is a pre-built image for an operating system in Amazon. Scroll down until to the Ubuntu option and click the Select button.

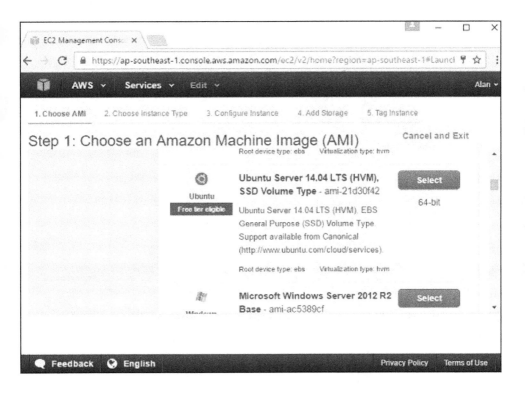

Step 7 – In the next screen, choose the configuration of the machine. Choose the General purpose – t2.micro option and then click the 'Next: Configure Instance Details' button.

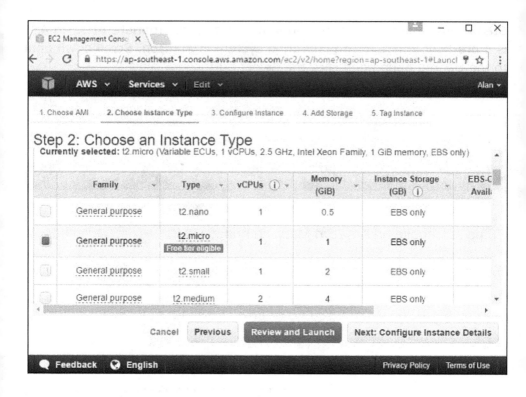

Step 8 – In the next screen, enter the following details as shown in the screenshot.

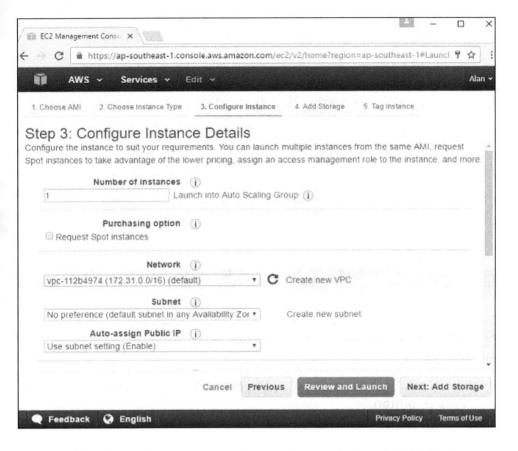

- The number of instances to launch – Keep 1 as the default.
- VPC – If there is no existing VPC, choose the option to create a new one.

Now, if we choose the option to create a new subnet, we need to perform the following sub steps.

Click the Create VPC button. (Note: The VPC is known as a virtual private network which is used to store all AWS objects in an isolated environment.)

In the Create VPC dialog box, enter the following details and click the 'Yes Create' button.

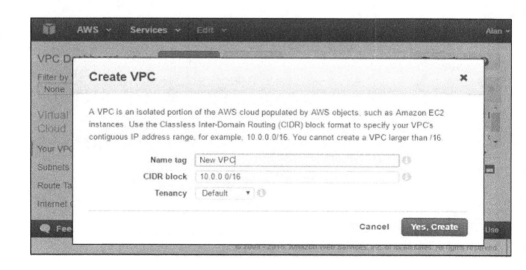

- For the subnet, keep the default setting as it is.

- For the Auto-assign Public IP option, choose 'use subnet setting(Enable)'.
- Keep the IAM Role as 'none'.
- Keep the Shutdown behavior as 'none'.
- The remaining settings can remain as by default.

Click the Next: Add Storage button.

Step 9 – In the next screen, keep the default storage as is and click the Review and Launch button.

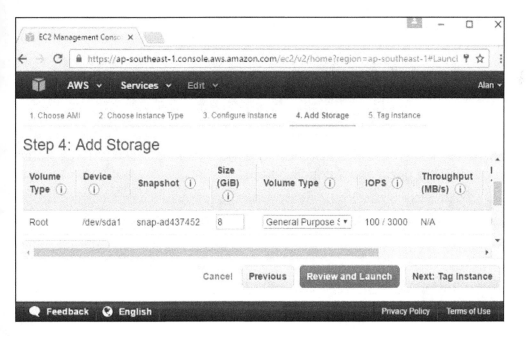

Step 10 – The review screen will pop up. Click the Launch button.

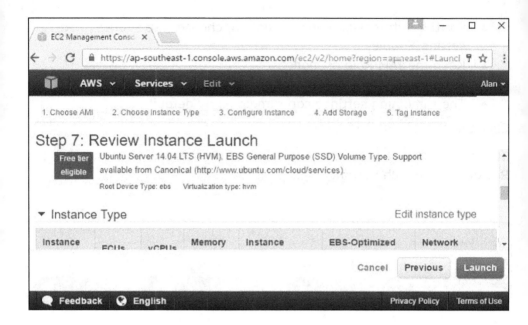

Step 11 — The next screen prompts to create a new key pair. This is required to log into the instance when it is created. Enter a key name and click the download Key pair button.

Step 12 – Once download is complete, click the Launch Instances button.

Step 13 – Click the 'View Instances' button.

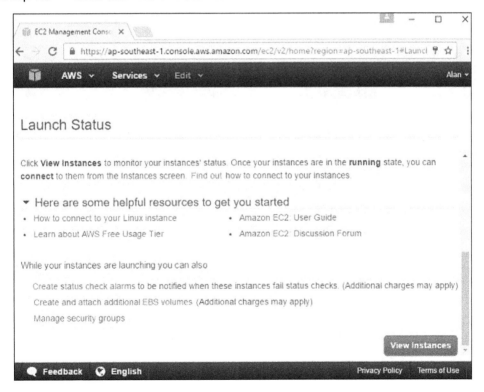

Step 14 — Once the state of the instance is running, click the Connect button.

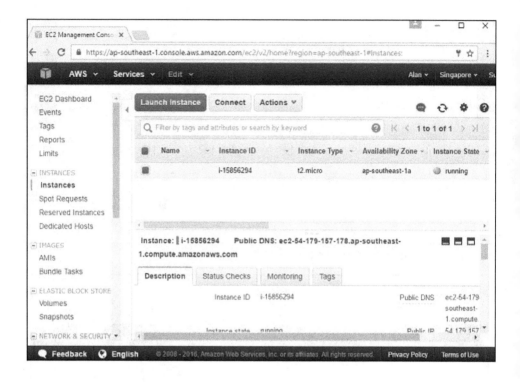

The next dialog box presents the steps to log into the Ubuntu server machine.

Step 15 – Perform the steps as we would normally do, using a SSH client to log into the machine.

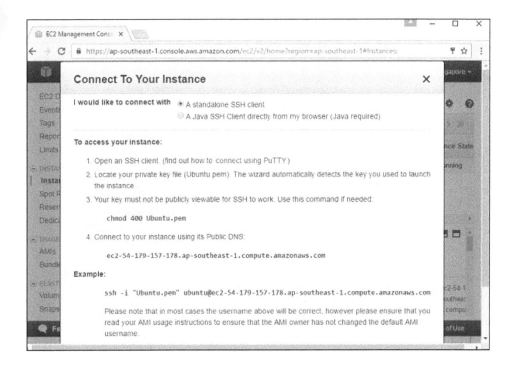

www.ingramcontent.com/pod-product-compliance
Lightning Source LLC
Chambersburg PA
CBHW071117050326
40690CB00008B/1255